JUDY

JUDY

The Films and Career
of JUDY GARLAND

by JOE MORELLA and
EDWARD Z. EPSTEIN

THE CITADEL PRESS

NEW YORK

Acknowledgments

We gratefully acknowledge the help of: Metro-Goldwyn-Mayer, Warner Brothers-Seven Arts, United Artists, Capitol Records, Twentieth Century-Fox, Columbia Pictures, Bill Doll Associates.

Also, Patrick B. Clark, Ted Goldsmith, Robert Hilburn, Wayne Martin, Robert Rosterman, Michael Scrimenti, John Springer, Paul Waigner.

And special thanks to Judith Crist, Arthur Freed, E. Y. Harburg, Gene Kelly, Joe Pasternak, and Senator George Murphy.

First paperbound edition, September 1970
Copyright © 1969 by Joe Morella and Edward Z. Epstein
All rights reserved
Published by Citadel Press, Inc.
A subsidiary of Lyle Stuart, Inc.
222 Park Avenue South, New York, N.Y. 10003
Published simultaneously in Canada by
George J. McLeod Limited
73 Bathurst St., Toronto 2B, Ontario
Manufactured in the United States of America
Designed by William Meinhardt
ISBN 0-8065-0206-1

For my Parents
and
Pat and Grams

For my Parents
and
Vivian and Steve

Contents

Introduction

by Judith Crist

The Hollywood star system, some experts hold, came a cropper when the studio publicists started turning the stars into the folks next door. But when the girl next door becomes a Hollywood star—ah, well.

For my generation, for those of us who adolesced and came of age with the movies of the Thirties and the Forties, Judy Garland was and will always be the girl next door who became a movie star and managed to survive the system. This wasn't a case of fan-mag mythology, of press agentry, of a manufactured studio bio; we were there, we saw it happen, we watched it all unfold step by step and we were glad for Judy and we laughed with Judy and we cried with Judy and we triumphed with her and we sorrowed and rejoiced and suffered and to this day we know she can do no wrong because she's all pro and all heart and we've lived our lives together and we can't give her anything but love. And there never was and there never will be another film star quite like her because there will never be another Hollywood like the one that created and used and abused her or another movie audience like the one that loved her. Nor is it likely that there will be another film star who could move from screen to stage with such professional ease and capture theater audiences around the world with that same charismatic appeal to the heart that turned the mass response of thousands at a time into an individualized affection.

It isn't easy to analyze the unique qualities of Judy Garland as movie star or cult-idol, so closely are they related to her personal qualities; indeed, the tragedy of her life may well be that she was all movie star and never had a chance to be a private person. Coming from vaudeville as a "little girl with a big voice," tabbed

right off the bat by Sophie Tucker herself as her probable successor as the Red Hot Mama of show biz, Judy Garland came to movies as a "natural," a song-and-dance actress who had never had formal training in singing, dancing or acting. As a child star she was no raving beauty: Ann Rutherford and Ava Gardner were the lovelies who got Mickey Rooney in the Andy Hardy pictures. Judy, somehow biggish-bosomed and thickish-waisted, albeit with lovely slim legs, with sort of hair-hair and a pert nose and—well, Judy was *real* and a good sport and—boy, how she could sing and dance and just be—well, like a girl you knew and liked and could talk to and be real *with*.

There it was—the timeless truth at the heart of Judy Garland's appeal throughout her career: the little girl lost, the wide-eyed good sport, the believer, the vulnerable creature who had nothing to see her through except her talents and her feelings, and those were put right out for all to see. No fake, no fraud, neither a false eyelash nor a false note, just the real thing from heart to head. And how could anyone, of any age, resist the appeal or fail to respond to the fun and the frolic and the joy and—ah yes, the quaver, the fine tremulous suggestion of vulnerability, the depth of feeling glimmering through that shining but never slick surface?

There are fashions in love goddesses, in vamps and villainesses,

in mother-images and sex symbols. But there is no fashion in talent and professionalism, and thus, from fifteen to twenty-eight, in some thirty films for M-G-M, and on into her thirties and forties (and ours) she developed those talents and polished her professionalism and we watched her grow on the screen, on stage, on television. From the kid serenading Clark Gable to Dorothy longing for over-the-rainbow happiness, from the youngster pitching in to put on a Depression-era show in the barn and making it in the Ziegfeld Follies to the ready-for-romance St. Louis charmer, from the pal who two-a-dayed with Mickey Rooney and was dazzled by the Broadway big-time to the gal who could not only keep in step with Gene Kelly and Fred Astaire but win them in romance, from the on-screen Oscar ceremonies that spelled personal tragedy to the harrowing witness-box of Nuremberg that symbolized world tragedy, Judy lived through the troubled times with us, always there, always contemporary, always on top of the material, always a reality for her public.

Bette Davis, Joan Crawford, Hedy Lamarr, even Lana Turner were all given us as grown-up ready-made stars, somehow, swathed in the ermines and diamonds of screen queens. But Judy was the girl from our block—and if we spotted her with jewels and furs we felt it was a dress-up occasion. And if, in her off-screen life, we

read of a domestic problem or heard rumbles of suspensions and
tensions—it was Judy in trouble because she was in thrall to a
heartless studio, Judy victimized by a system, Judy fighting off the
rigors of diet and overwork and nervous strain. It was Judy in
top hat and mini-tux, the long lovely black-stockinged limbs never
changing; it was Judy in Oz, really believing through it all that
there's no place like home; it was Judy, smudge-faced and perspiring
after the "Couple of Swells" tramp number, sitting on the edge
of the stage at the Palace or Palladium or Metropolitan Opera
House and taking us over the rainbow to the purity of heart
we all once knew.

We remember Judy young and happy and a marvel of vitality
and charm—and we think we all must have been that way; we see
her in her latter years and we know that we've all been through
a lot but not quite the way she has. And there it is—not the
Red Hot Mama Miss Tucker envisioned—the girl next door who
became a movie star and who never moved away, but stayed right
there so we could share it all with her. And we did. All the way.
Some of us wound up fans, some made a cult of Judy-worship—
but all of us are marked by a singular experience, of having cared
about the person as well as the personality. And the evocation
thereof is uniquely Judy Garland's.

A snapshot, circa 1936

JUDY: *Born in a Trunk*

1935. Franklin D. Roosevelt was President of the United States.
The country was in the depths of a depression, the most critical
in its history, and the international situation, then as now, was in
a precariously explosive state.

There supposedly weren't any spare pennies in the pockets of the
public for the purpose of entertainment, but the motion picture
business was bigger than ever, and growing at a fantastic rate.
The top ten box-office stars in the nation that year were
Shirley Temple, Will Rogers, Clark Gable, Fred Astaire and
Ginger Rogers, Joan Crawford, Claudette Colbert, Dick Powell,
Wallace Beery, Joe E. Brown, and James Cagney.

Baby Shirley Temple was the child-goddess of the cinema—
a golden-curled, forget-your-troubles, celluloid angel worshipped by
a suffering populace which could, momentarily at least, escape from
its problems into the lollipop world of Movieland. And Shirley's
box-office magic had all the movie studios searching for child stars
with similar potential.

At this time the largest motion picture studio in the world was
Metro-Goldwyn-Mayer, the home of such screen luminaries as
Clark Cable, Joan Crawford, Greta Garbo, Wallace Beery, and
many others. The man who ran this studio was the Mayer of
M-G-M—legendary movie mogul Louis B. Mayer.

A man with an uncanny ability to determine what the public
would buy in entertainment, it was Mayer in 1935 who auditioned
a plump, pretty, thirteen-year-old, vaudeville-trained singer named
Judy Garland. After hearing Judy sing, he promptly signed her

*An autographed publicity portrait,
about 1937*

to a contract, without making her take a screen or sound test—
the only time in the history of M-G-M that a player was signed
without a test. When Mayer signed Judy to a contract, he did so
without having a particular role in mind for her.

Within less than five years, little Judy Garland would be firmly
established as one of the biggest box-office draws in motion pictures,
and one of M-G-M's all-time moneymakers.

Ironically, Judy was second choice for the starring role in the
film which marked the turning point in her career and catapulted
her to stardom of the first magnitude, M-G-M's *The Wizard of Oz*.
Metro originally wanted to borrow Shirley Temple from 20th
Century-Fox, but had to "settle" for Garland when the studios
could not agree on terms.

Judy would maintain her star status through the years, despite
illness and heartbreak, and scale even loftier peaks of success long
after her contemporaries—including her benefactor, Mr. Mayer—
would be leafing through scrapbooks of glories gone by. She would
become a legend in her own time, living countless real-life dramas
exceeding any role she would play in any of her films.

It is appropriate that many of Judy's early films had her playing
a vaudevillian, since her parents, Ethel Marian (Milne) and
Frank Avent Gumm, were vaudeville players.

Born Frances Gumm on June 10, 1922, in Grand Rapids,
Minnesota, Judy had an early introduction to show business.

Judy and her mother in 1941

Her father, at that time manager of the New Theatre in Grand
Rapids, had occasionally been presenting his two older daughters,
Judy's sisters Virginia and Mary Jane, on stage to sing duets.
They were accompanied on the piano by their mother.

When Judy was three, she disobeyed her parents' instructions to
remain quietly backstage while her sisters were performing.
Judy reported years later: "My debut at the age of three was an
indication of what was to come. It was amateur night at my
father's theatre and I wanted to sing before the audience. . . .
Even then I was a very determined little girl. I ran on stage and
sang 'Jingle Bells,' and not only once. I kept singing chorus after
chorus until Dad marched out on the stage and carried me off."

In 1927, when Judy was five (Virginia and Mary Jane were
seven and twelve, respectively), the Gumms moved to Lancaster,
California. Judy had hay fever, and her parents thought the change
in climate would be good for her allergy.

Mrs. Gumm formed an act for the girls, accompanying them on
the piano. The youthful singing trio reportedly made its debut
at the Biltmore Hotel in Los Angeles, and received the important
sum of $1.50 for the engagement.

The girls were enrolled in public schools, and Judy participated
in school recitals and plays, which led to work with the Meglin
Kiddies, a bevy of tots that played theatres throughout California.
Judy's solo consisted of her singing "I Can't Give You Anything

But Love, Baby," and when the Meglin troupe reached Los Angeles, talent executive and producer Gus Edwards was impressed with young Miss Gumm's exceptional talent. He went backstage to congratulate her, and the older Gumm girls, who had given up stage performing to concentrate on school, were encouraged by Mr. Edward's reaction to Frances. His enthusiasm prompted them to re-enter show business.

When Mr. Gumm's health began to fail, the child singing trio became the main support of the Gumm family. The sisters, with their mother, toured the principal cities of the United States, but were never considered by vaudeville bookers as more than "third rate." Detroit was the closest they came to New York, and Judy, still Frances Gumm, was billed as "the little girl with the great big voice."

In 1931, when Judy was nine, the first "big break" came. The Gumms got a booking at an important theatre, Chicago's Oriental, and were very excited over their prospects upon arriving in the Windy City. They went to the theatre, where the marquee blazoned the name of the show's headliner, George Jessel. And also on the marquee was their name: "The Glum Sisters."

They were heartbroken at the misspelling. Jessel had the management correct the mistake, but considered it "no improvement." He suggested they change their name to Garland (Jessel's close friend was the then drama critic of the New York *World-Telegram*, Robert Garland), thereby keeping the first initial of their real name.

They accepted the suggestion. *Variety's* review of the act stated that "the youngest . . . handles ballads like a veteran and gets every note and word over with a personality that hits audiences. Her sisters merely form a background."

Frances decided to change her first name to Judy about a year later. Her mother didn't like the name, but Judy did. She thought

*At her wedding to Vincente Minnelli,
her second husband: Left to right,
Ira Gershwin, Minnelli, Judy, Louis
B. Mayer, and Betty Asher*

it sounded "peppy," and also she liked the song "Judy,"
Hoagy Carmichael's popular song of that day.

In 1934, they returned to Los Angeles to get bookings, to be
near Mr. Gumm, who was still ill. However, the Garland Sisters
were no more successful than the Gumm Sisters, and the act broke
up when one of them got married. Judy continued as a single at
the urging of her mother, who was certain all Judy needed was
"the lucky break."

Judy got an engagement at Lake Tahoe (a reviewer described
her voice as "poignant and unforgettable") and was heard by
Lew Brown (of the songwriting team of DeSylva, Brown and
Henderson). He suggested to Mrs. Gumm that she try to get the
youngster into films, and the suggestion fell on willing ears.

Shortly after the Louis B. Mayer audition, and the signing by
M-G-M, tragedy struck hard at Judy—her father died. His death
was a deep blow, as she loved him dearly.

Vincente Minnelli and daughter Liza

*With Arthur Freed, Louis B. Mayer,
and Irving Berlin in 1948*

Judy first appeared on screen in a 1936 two-reel short, *Every Sunday,* along with another youngster under contract to M-G-M, Deanna Durbin. It is interesting to note that Mayer, who was partial to operatic-type singers (for example, Jeanette MacDonald, Kathryn Grayson, Jane Powell), allowed Durbin's option to drop, while renewing Garland's. It was later suggested that this was a glaring error in judgment, since Durbin became a top box-office star soon after at Universal, while Garland languished at M-G-M with nothing much happening for her.

Judy was lent to 20th Century-Fox in 1936 for her first full-length picture, *Pigskin Parade.* The following year marked her first real success at Metro. Music arranger Roger Edens had written special lyrics for the song "You Made Me Love You," and suggested that Judy sing it to "The King" at a special birthday party the studio was giving for Clark Gable. Judy's rendition of the number was so successful that the studio decided to work it into their big musical, *Broadway Melody of 1938,* released in 1937.

In that film, Garland was cast as a youngster being pushed into show business by her stage mother, portrayed by Sophie Tucker. In the film, Judy sang "Dear Mr. Gable, You Made Me Love You." The song and Judy were a smash. *The New York Times* described Judy's sequence as "probably the greatest tour de force in recent screen history."

While Sophie Tucker played Judy's stage mother on screen, Ethel Marian Milne Gumm was in fact living the role. Judy's relationship with her mother was, as far as the public was concerned, a happy one. Judy herself, however, has said: "Mother was the real-life wicked witch of the west. . . . Mother . . . was no good for anything except to create chaos and fear.

Danny Kaye and Robert Christenberry present Judy with a silver union card, representing life membership in seven theatrical unions (1951).

She didn't like me because of my talent. . . . She had a crude voice and my sisters had lousy voices too. . . . When I review my financial problems, I have to admit they began with my mother."

Until Judy's first marriage, her mother accompanied her everywhere. Mrs. Gumm was undoubtedly a strong influence in Judy's life.

In 1937, following *Broadway Melody,* Judy was cast for the first time opposite Mickey Rooney, in *Thoroughbreds Don't Cry.* It was to mark the beginning of a long, successful on-screen partnership, and a lifetime friendship. They appeared together in eight subsequent films and countless stage shows and personal appearances. Mickey Rooney was a partner Judy said she enjoyed

With Bing Crosby, rehearsing for a radio show in 1952

Arriving at Grand Central Station in 1954 with her third husband Sidney Luft and daughter Liza Minnelli

working with because each knew exactly what the other was going to do. She has said that he was her favorite co-star.

Metro gave Garland exposure and experience in several more films in the late '30's, in which she had the opportunity of working with such professionals as Fanny Brice, Allan Jones, Mary Astor, and Walter Pidgeon.

Judy's stock continued to rise, and in 1939 *The Wizard of Oz* firmly established her as a major star and provided her with the Academy Award-winning song that has been her trademark, "Over the Rainbow." Garland and Rooney were sent to New York to perform in person, on the stage of the Capitol Theatre, in conjunction with the film's premiere. They caused a sensation, and the movie was an unqualified smash.

The Wizard of Oz is now considered a classic, and enjoys tremendous success via its yearly exposure on nation-wide television, winning new generations of fans for Garland.

Judy won a special Academy Award for *The Wizard of Oz,* for the "best juvenile performance of the year." She was promoted to adult roles, starting with *Babes in Arms* (1939), which again teamed her with Mickey Rooney.

Judy's tendency to gain weight was kept rigidly under control, and the studio put her on a strict diet and a gymnasium exercise routine. The cycle of gaining and losing weight has continued to plague her throughout her life. Many people contend that the persistent use of diet pills, sleeping pills, and stimulants during her youth started her on the collision course she was to follow for many years.

On the basis of *The Wizard of Oz* and *Babes in Arms,* in 1940 Judy was voted one of the top ten box-office attractions by theatre-owners throughout the nation. She was the only female on the list besides Bette Davis.

That same year she starred in *Andy Hardy Meets Debutante, Strike Up the Band,* and *Little Nelly Kelly.*

Little Nelly Kelly teamed her with George Murphy, a friend she has kept through the years. She played a dual role in this film, in which she had the one and only death scene of her career. As always, her performance met with critical approval and her stature as a dramatic actress continued to grow.

While studio publicity announced the fact that Judy would play her first love scene in *Little Nelly Kelly,* Judy announced her engagement to orchestra leader David Rose, ex-husband of Martha Raye. The studio and Judy's mother were not happy, but Judy ignored their objections and married Rose on June 10, 1941.

After three films in 1941, Judy reached a new peak with her beautiful performance in the 1942 film, *For Me and My Gal.* This was the first picture in which Garland was the only star billed above the title. Her co-stars were George Murphy and newcomer Gene Kelly.

Working at a fantastic pace, Judy was not only making movies but also doing personal appearances, starring on radio, and making records. In December, 1942, CBS's "Lux Radio Theatre" presented an adaptation of *A Star Is Born*, starring Judy, Walter Pidgeon, and Adolphe Menjou. Judy loved the role, and would play it on the screen years later. (Judy also starred on "The Lux Radio Theatre" in *Strike Up the Band* and *Merton of the Movies*, both with Mickey Rooney, and *Morning Glory*, with John Payne and Adolphe Menjou.)

It was wartime, and Judy made an extensive USO tour before returning to moviemaking. Her marriage to Rose faltered, but her career continued at a phenomenal pace, hitting a new high in 1944 with *Meet Me in St. Louis*, in which she was directed for the first time by Vincente Minnelli. A film depicting turn-of-the-century America, it provided Garland with one of her most memorable roles. The score for the film included "The Trolley Song," "The Boy Next Door," "Have Yourself a Merry Little Christmas," and, of course, the title song.

Meet Me in St. Louis was one of the all-time box-office hits for M-G-M and Garland. She had reached the peak. Judy Garland was earning $5000 a week, and her name was box-office magic.

The Clock, her next film and only straight dramatic role for M-G-M, was also directed by Minnelli. On June 15, 1945, a week after her divorce from Rose became final, Judy married Minnelli, and a year later their daughter Liza was born.

Campaigning for John F. Kennedy in 1960

Hit followed hit. *The Harvey Girls, Ziegfeld Follies of 1946,* and *Till the Clouds Roll By.* Seemingly, Judy's personal life was happy, but deep-seated problems were surfacing.

In 1948, Judy starred with Gene Kelly in *The Pirate*, directed by Minnelli (it was not the usual Garland blockbuster at the box office), and the smash hit, *Easter Parade*. Fred Astaire was called "out of retirement" to replace Gene Kelly in this film. Kelly had broken an ankle during a dance rehearsal.

At this time, Judy was not in the best of health. She was suffering from nervous exhaustion and had to withdraw from *The Barkleys of Broadway*, in which M-G-M wanted to re-team her with Astaire. Ginger Rogers took over the role, re-uniting her with her famed partner for the first time in ten years.

Judy came back to work in 1948, and was featured for the last time on screen with Mickey Rooney in a short sequence for M-G-M's all-star musical, *Words and Music*. In this film, she looked thin and drawn.

She managed to complete Joe Pasternak's production of *In the Good Old Summertime,* a success for Metro during the 1949 season. It was reported that her mental and physical condition caused many delays in production. Producer Pasternak said in his book, *Easy the Hard Way:* "There was never a word uttered in recrimination when she was late, didn't show up, or couldn't go on. Those of us who worked with her knew her magical genius and respected it."

This was a period when the inroads of television started to affect the motion picture industry. The studios were tightening their belts. The days of temperamental stars and exorbitant production costs were coming to a close.

With children Joey and Lorna Luft

M-G-M bought Irving Berlin's Broadway hit *Annie Get Your Gun* specifically as a vehicle for Garland. They paid more money for it than for any property they had bought up to that time. Busby Berkeley, who had directed many of her early musicals, was set to direct. Judy hadn't enjoyed working with Berkeley in the past and insisted he be replaced. She was adamant and walked out on the film until the studio complied. Charles Walters took over the direction.

She pre-recorded her songs for *Annie*. But she wasn't well, and didn't keep up with the production schedule. Although M-G-M's investment up to that time was estimated at over a million dollars, Judy was removed from the film, suspended, and sent to a Boston clinic. Betty Hutton was borrowed from Paramount to replace her.

After three months, Judy returned from suspension and starred for Metro in *Summer Stock*. It took six months to make this musical. Judy's weight fluctuated to such an extent that it was easily discernible on screen that she was much heavier in the early scenes of the film, and slimmed down considerably as it progressed. *Summer Stock* was a success, but it was to be her last film for M-G-M.

The studio cast her in *Royal Wedding,* to replace June Allyson, who was pregnant. But Judy, again ill and exhausted, caused production delays and was suspended for the second time in less than a year. Jane Powell replaced her as Fred Astaire's co-star.

Despondent over her suspension, Judy Garland shocked the world when, on June 20, 1950, she tried to commit suicide. The image of M-G-M's all-American darling was shattered forever when Judy shattered a water tumbler and tried to slash her throat.

The wound was superficial, but the act was indicative of the deep-seated troubles that had afflicted Miss Garland for years. The adverse publicity was the final straw. M-G-M announced that Judy was released from her contract.

Judy's mother moved back to Hollywood to be near her famous daughter. Though they had been estranged throughout the '40's, they were reunited briefly during this critical period in Judy's life, but by 1953 at the time of her death, Mrs. Gumm, now Mrs. Gilmore, was again estranged from Judy.

Judy Garland left Hollywood and started divorce proceedings against Vincente Minnelli in 1951. Her movie career seemed to be at an end. At about this time she met Michael Sidney Luft, who became her manager and persuaded her to play a four-week personal appearance engagement at the London Palladium for $20,000 a week.

Luft, a one-time test pilot and ex-husband of actress Lynn Bari, was a familiar Hollywood figure who had produced a few "B" pictures. He provided Judy with the confidence she lacked at the time, and the Palladium engagement was a ringing success.

The Palladium triumph led to Judy's famous return to vaudeville as the headliner at New York's Palace Theatre, where she broke all box-office records by extending her four-week engagement to nineteen weeks and grossing more than $750,000. The Garland cult, as we know it today, was now crystallized. Her loyal movie-going public now became her loyal concert-going public, and would remain faithful for years to come.

Judy and Luft were married in June, 1952, and in November of that year their daughter Lorna was born. (Another child, Joseph Wiley Luft, was born to them in March, 1955.)

Riding the crest of what was to be her first "comeback," Judy and her husband formed a production company to film the re-make

Receiving a gold record for the first 2-record album to reach the million-dollar mark in sales ("Judy at Carnegie Hall")

With Jack L. Warner (left) and Sophie Tucker at the Cocoanut Grove after the premiere of A Star Is Born *in 1954*

of *A Star Is Born,* in conjunction with Warner Brothers Pictures. Production delays made news as the film ran weeks behind schedule and way over budget. But *A Star Is Born,* finally released in October, 1954, was a critical success and Judy was nominated for an Academy Award for her performance as an actress whose career rose as her famous actor-husband's declined. James Mason and Charles Bickford co-starred with her in this film.

Judy made her television debut in 1955, on a CBS TV special, "The Ford Star Jubilee." Garland proved she could attract a huge audience to the small screen, as she had to the large.

In 1956, Luft and Judy began to make headlines with their marital difficulties. Friends said the breakup resulted from financial problems due to Luft's interest in horse racing. After a brief separation, they were re-united. Judy made sporadic concert and night club appearances. Her figure ballooned, but her voice retained its thrilling quality, and Judy's public remained faithful throughout this somewhat stagnant period of her career.

Unfavorable publicity resulted when Judy and *New York Herald Tribune* columnist Marie Torre became entangled in a legal battle in 1957. Judy had filed suit against CBS for allegedly breaking a contract. Miss Torre was indicted, convicted for contempt of court, and sent to jail, when she refused to reveal the source of an item she printed about Miss Garland and the CBS suit.

Additional unfavorable publicity concerning Judy's marital, professional, and financial problems continued to make news throughout the late '50's. Her career seemed on the wane, and her estrangement from Luft seemed final.

But again, a "comeback" was not far off. Freddie Fields and David Begelman became her agent-managers, and in January, 1961, she was signed to return to films in Stanley Kramer's all-star production, *Judgment at Nuremberg*. She had a small but key role and received star billing. Judy played a young German hausfrau accused by the Nazis of having an affair with an elderly Jew. Her performance won an Academy Award nomination as Best Supporting Actress of the Year.

Also in 1961, she enjoyed what was perhaps the greatest concert success of her career to date, an appearance at Carnegie Hall. This produced her recorded-on-the-scene Capitol album, "Judy at Carnegie Hall." The album was a smash, and a new Garland boom was launched. The Garland Cult had a resurgence, and even "non-believers" joined the group of loyal Garland fans welcoming a much slimmer Judy back again.

Her friends Frank Sinatra and Dean Martin joined her in a highly successful TV special on the CBS network in 1962. That year she completed two films: *A Child Is Waiting*, Stanley Kramer's production dealing with retarded children, in which she co-starred with Burt Lancaster, and *I Could Go on Singing* (originally titled *The Lonely Stage*). This was her first cinema musical since *A Star Is Born* and her first and only film to date made outside the United States.

In addition, she was the on-screen voice of the cartoon character Mewsette, in the UPA-Warner Brothers animated feature, *Gay Purr-ee*. Robert Goulet was the voice of Mewsette's boy friend. Despite decent reviews, none of these three films enjoyed the success at the box office of previous Garland movies.

Judy fought a bitter child custody battle with Sid Luft during the filming of *I Could Go on Singing*. It was an ordeal, and she was hospitalized for exhaustion.

Her eagerly awaited multi-million-dollar network television series debuted on CBS in 1963. There was much behind-the-scenes hassling, and the show was not successful in the ratings. It was canceled before the end of its initial season.

As she had done in 1951 after she left M-G-M, Judy, tired and disappointed by the failure of her television show, returned to London where she made a successful appearance with her daughter Liza at the Palladium. It was the first time Liza had formally worked with her mother. Describing that experience, Liza has said: "I'll never be afraid to perform with anyone ever again after that terrifying experience. . . . Mama at this point suddenly realized that she had a grown-up daughter. . . . She wasn't a kid *herself* any more. She became very competitive with me."

Arriving in Sydney, Australia, in 1964, with her fourth husband, Mark Herron (left)

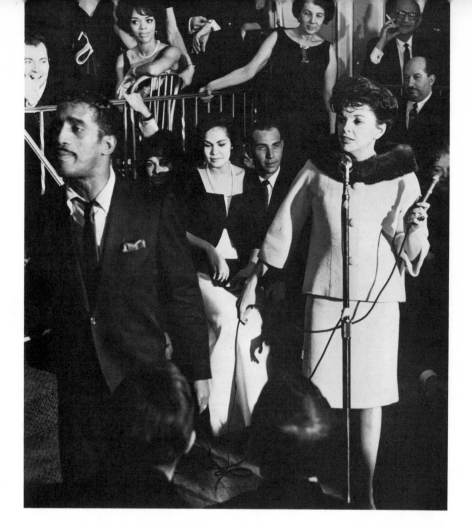

With Sammy Davis, Jr., at the Cue *Awards in 1964*

At a later date, appearing as a surprise guest at the Palladium on the same bill with the Beatles, who were then enjoying the first flush of their phenomenal popularity, Judy was a sensation and literally stole the show. She sang "Over the Rainbow" and was received with an ovation that dwarfed any that had come before her appearance that evening or would come after.

Judy traveled around the world, and at about this time—the summer of 1964—legal entanglements clouded the issue as to whether she was legally married to 36-year-old Mark Herron. He was identified as an actor and her traveling companion. As it turned out, her divorce from Sid Luft did not become final until November, 1965. She then legally married Herron in Las Vegas on November 14, 1965. They separated six months later, and were divorced in April, 1967. It was her fourth marriage.

After her return to the States, Judy continued working, making several guest appearances on television. Then 20th Century-Fox, where Judy had filmed *Pigskin Parade* in 1936, when she was fourteen, pulled a casting coup and announced they had signed Judy Garland for a starring role in their eagerly anticipated production of the best-seller *Valley of the Dolls*. One of the characters in the story, being played by another actress, bore a strong resemblance to the real-life Judy Garland.

Newspapers throughout the world carried the story that Garland was again returning to motion pictures. She would portray the aging musical comedy star Helen Lawson in *Valley of the Dolls*, and would sing one song in the film.

Judy did not appear in *Valley of the Dolls*. After a long series of delays, Fox announced that she would be replaced by Susan Hayward.

Her marriage to Herron over, Judy announced her engagement to a young publicist, Tom Green. (Their marriage did not materialize.) Her career seemed in the doldrums. But, as in the past, success was once again around the corner.

In late 1967, under the aegis of her ex-husband Sid Luft, Judy played a spectacularly successful four-week engagement at the Palace Theatre in New York. She signed a new recording contract with ABC-Paramount Records, and the Palace engagement was commemorated with an album, "Judy at the Palace." The recording did not enjoy the success of her "Judy at Carnegie Hall" album, but there was no doubt that Judy Garland was still a big box-office attraction.

Following her Palace engagement, she went on to Boston, where she established a new attendance record when more than 100,000 people turned out for her outdoor concert. However, ensuing engagements in other cities were not as successful, and she returned to New York, where she played the Felt Forum of the new Madison Square Garden. In the summer of 1968, she appeared in concert at the Garden State Arts Center in New Jersey.

Christmas of that year found Judy engaged again, this time to 35-year-old singer and night club manager Mickey Deans. They were married in January in London, where Judy fulfilled a successful—but somewhat controversial—singing engagement at the "Talk of the Town" night club. Reportedly ill with influenza, she was often late for her nightly performances and sometimes had to cope with belligerent audiences.

What's next for Judy?

In recent appearances she has introduced her children, Lorna and Joey, as entertainers. All Miss Garland's children are talented, but none possesses the magical quality of the Rainbow Girl.

Her concert appearances are less frequent now. However, the career of the seemingly indestructible star is constantly regenerated via the sale of her records and the programming of her movies on television.

As this book goes to press, Judy Garland is 46 years old, although many people think she is much older, since she has been a major star for so many years. She has earned and spent millions of dollars, and entertained and brightened the lives of countless millions of people.

There are no movie roles in sight for Judy at the moment, but the pattern of her life, if graphed, would form an incredible zig-zag of Ups and Downs. One would not—or should not—be astonished to read tomorrow that Judy Garland has been signed to play an important film role, or has set a new house record with a concert appearance.

Another comeback? To quote Judy:

"What comeback? I've never been away!"

A recent airport departure shot

The Judy I Know

Comments by
ARTHUR FREED, E. Y. HARBURG,
GENE KELLY, SENATOR GEORGE MURPHY,
and JOE PASTERNAK

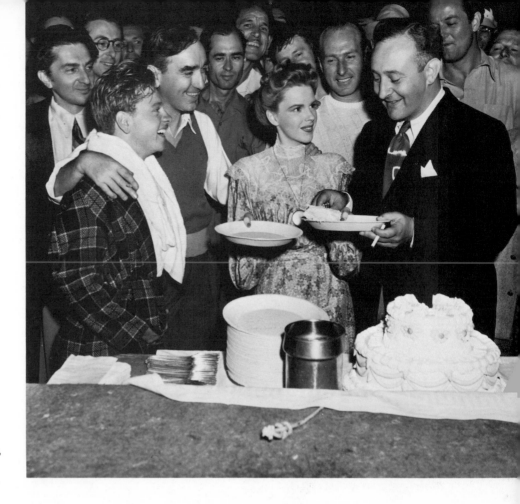

With Mickey Rooney, Busby Berkeley,
and Arthur Freed

The Judy I Know

Arthur Freed

ARTHUR FREED is one of Hollywood's leading producers of
musicals. He is a past president of the Academy of Motion
Picture Arts and Sciences; a two-time Academy Award winner,
and recipient of the distinguished Irving Thalberg Award.

In addition to the fourteen films he produced which starred
Judy Garland, he also produced *An American in Paris,*
Singin' in the Rain, Gigi, and a score of others. Also known
as a top song writer, his great hits include "Singin' in the
Rain," "You Were Meant For Me," and "I Cried For You."

Mr. Freed is currently preparing a new film, *Say It With*
Music, which will feature the music of Irving Berlin.

The first time I met Judy she was with her two sisters, and they
gave an audition. Roger Edens and Jack Robbins, the music
publisher, were also there. Judy's mother played piano, and she
played pretty bad piano. I heard them sing two or three songs,
and I finally said let me hear the little girl sing alone. Judy sang
"Zing Went the Strings of My Heart." She was a "natural."

She could learn a song faster than anybody I ever knew, with less
rehearsal. The musicians loved working with her.

Arthur Freed

Judy's vaudeville background was a help, but she didn't have long career in vaudeville, and bigtime vaudeville was already finished by the time she got started. Judy is basically the product of motion pictures.

———

Some child actors are like child artists. They're wonderful until they improve. And then they improve into failures. There are only a few exceptions—for example, Judy, Elizabeth Taylor, Julie Andrews. Some children have a quality of innocence and reality that you can believe. But they lose that, except in rare cases. Judy is the prime example of the child star who made it.

———

At M-G-M, we had what was known as the Freed unit. In that, Judy was the star. There was Roger Edens and Kay Thompson and Bob Alton, the choreographer—many people, and it was like a

On the Meet Me in St. Louis *set: Left to right, Lucille Bremer, Leon Ames, Mary Astor, Joan Carroll, Vincente Minnelli, Judy, Arthur Freed, Harry Davenport, Margaret O'Brien, and Henry Daniels, Jr.*

family. My relationship with Judy was always warm and affectionate. We had a good time making a picture.

In her films, Judy was always absolutely contemporary. No film that Judy Garland made for M-G-M ever lost money. Her appeal was national, not just regional.

———

What makes Judy Garland tick? Judy Garland! You can't explain or analyze what makes her tick—she just does. This girl for fifteen years or more had no equal. There's nobody since Al Jolson who can handle an audience—walk down to the footlights and sit down and talk to an audience—and hold them the way Judy does. She could sit down in the audience, peel a banana and eat it and they would love her.

She gets into the hearts of people. Judy interprets a lyric as very few people in our business ever do. It takes people like Fred Astaire, Frank Sinatra, Bing Crosby and Julie Andrews to interpret lyrics. Judy had—and has—her own style and sang her way into the hearts of everyone in the audience. And everybody backstage, too.

———

Judy never felt any lack of confidence in doing a song or doing a picture. But in her personal life, I think she did. What went wrong with Judy was not in her professional life. It was something within her private emotions. Judy was always a romantic by her very nature. She's a natural actress because you believe her, and that's what an actress is—someone you believe. But I think she had a terrific inferiority complex as a person. Now that's a guess, I'm not a psychiatrist.

———

Judy is not an intellectual, but she's very wise. She has a great deal of wisdom, and there's not a mean bone in Judy's body. In all the years I've known her, I've never known her to do a mean thing to anybody. She's a wonderful mother, and always wanted the children with her. They have great affection for her.

———

Judy had no sense of money. Yet in another sense, she always worried about security, but never did anything about it.

Arthur Freed

E. Y. Harburg

The Judy I Know

E. Y. Harburg

E. Y. "YIP" HARBURG is one of the most distinguished lyric writers of our time. He wrote the lyrics for *Finian's Rainbow, Bloomer Girl* and the motion picture *Cabin in the Sky.* "Brother Can You Spare a Dime" and "Happiness Is Just a Thing Called Joe" are among his score of hits. Mr. Harburg wrote the lyrics, and Harold Arlen the music, for the song which will be forever linked with Judy Garland—"Over the Rainbow."

I worked along with Noel Langley on the script for *The Wizard of Oz.* My job as a lyricist was to develop and write songs which would fit the characters. Here was Dorothy, a little girl from Kansas, a bleak place where there were no flowers, where there was no color of any kind. What does a child like this want? The only thing colorful in her world was a rainbow.

Also, the girl longed for something more than her drab existence. This yearning—part of the human condition—we wanted to work into the song. We discussed all this and Harold Arlen came up with a beautiful melody. We decided on "Over the Rainbow" as the title. It was a musical expression of these emotional yearnings and what motivated Dorothy into the dream.

At first I was stuck with the first two notes. Now, of course, it seems simple. But before I'd decided on "somewhere," it was difficult.

Judy was an unusual child, with an ability to project a song and a voice that penetrated your insides. She sang not just to your ears, but to your tear ducts. Just like a great cantor, she combined the superb voice with an understanding of the music and lyrics and this

[30]

ability to sing into your soul. She was the most unusual voice in the first half of this century.

———

When she started, Judy was the greatest. As a child, she sang with all the naturalness and clarity of a child. Now, singers are artificial—all goo, embroidery and gimmicks—they have no connection between the words and the music, between the human and humanity. They cannot communicate honest emotion.

———

Honesty, not phoniness, moves people. Judy Garland was to singing what Gershwin's music was to music. They brought a quality and vitality that was typically and uniquely American.

———

The American fantasy called success eluded Judy. Making a film is grueling excitement every minute. It is an unnatural environment. She had no life—no vacations—she was there to be applauded and toasted every minute. She had only tinsel, nothing real.

———

In Hollywood, Judy was a commodity. She was there for exploitation. When they saw they had a moneymaker, they used her to the hilt—unwisely and inhumanly, with no conception of the psychological treatment of a human being. This was common in the industry. If a star was box-office one year, that didn't mean he would be box-office the next. So the studio wanted every ounce of profit they could get.

———

Judy's problem is that she lets others handle her career. If she judged for herself, she'd be okay. She's a natural and needs no guidance musically. She just needs some editing and guidance in selecting her songs. You can't kill a talent like Judy's. Only bad material can do that.

With Ray Bolger and Jack Haley in
The Wizard of Oz, *for which Harburg*
wrote the lyrics

The Judy I Know

Gene Kelly

GENE KELLY, the legendary dancer-singer-actor currently devoting his talents to film directing *(Hello Dolly!)*, starred in three pictures with Judy Garland—*For Me and My Gal, The Pirate* and *Summer Stock*.

I had seen all of Judy's early pictures quite awhile before coming to Hollywood. She was without peer. I didn't know Judy until she had already been married to David Rose, but in this early period of her marriage she did change and mature professionally and I saw a great deal of this happen.

Judy was a good dancer, but not a fine one. Her ability here was to take a group of steps or a routine beyond her capacities and somehow give it an authenticity and authority that made her look a far better dancer than she was technically.

With Gene Kelly in Summer Stock

Gene Kelly

With Gene Kelly in The Pirate

You can't define charisma, but she had it always. The amazing thing about her talent was the swiftness with which she could grasp and interpret things that would take other people (and I mean talented people) ten times as long to catch.

———

The Garland cult? To begin, I believe that Judy's long career was a contributing factor, perhaps a major one. Don't forget she started out as a child with great talent and took several generations along with her, always improving that talent and adding to the increasing mobs of idolizers.

But even all this makes too much sense. When you get down to the incredible Garland cult, you just have to use that abused word *charisma*.

———

Judy has fierce loves and fierce hates, but in her love she is loyal. She has also had so many difficulties here and there, that *her* loyal friends like to help her if they can, and like to keep loving her.

With George Murphy
in Little Nelly Kelly

The Judy I Know

Senator George Murphy

GEORGE MURPHY, now a distinguished Senator from California, was one of Hollywood's leading musical stars. He starred opposite Judy Garland in three Metro-Goldwyn-Mayer films: *Broadway Melody of 1938, Little Nelly Kelly* and *For Me and My Gal.*

I saw her first when she was part of a sister team known as the Gumm Sisters, and I was amazed at the great talent of this little girl who sat up on a piano and did an imitation of the great Helen Morgan that was absolutely unbelievable. I have never forgotten that. There was a style and a maturity and a capability about her performance that one seldom finds in a much older and more experienced person. As Judy developed, it didn't seem to be a complete change. As far as I'm concerned all that happened was that she got a little older, much more attractive, stopped walking pigeon-toed, and her talent increased with her years.

And I recall the wonderful pictures Judy made with Mickey Rooney and how the efforts of these two fine stars practically kept that great studio running for a couple of years.

I have always said that I believe that Judy had one of the most complete and limitless talents of anyone that I have ever known in show business, and in my judgment there is absolutely no part— musical, non-musical, comedy, tragedy or anything in between— that she couldn't do as well if not better than anyone else.

I think that the so-called Garland cult is maybe what we just used to call a Garland fan club or a group of Garland followers, and I think that this has been building over the years for the reasons that I have stated above, and because she continues to absolutely electrify audiences in a manner that no one else quite matches.

I have always said from the first time I saw her that she has the great quality of making one want to cry and laugh almost at the same time. There was always an underlying tragic feeling about Judy.

I have never known Judy to do anything that wasn't kind or thoughtful or considerate to any of her fellow performers. She has always been a warm friend and in return that usually attracts complete friendship; and the high regard and respect that all have for her tremendous and endless talent is merely a reflection of the usual honest appraisal that show people have for one another.

I used to call her Grandma when she was a little girl. . . .

With George Murphy
in For Me and My Gal

The Judy I Know

Joe Pasternak

Joe Pasternak is a widely known and highly successful motion picture producer. At Universal in 1936, he starred Deanna Durbin in her initial film hits. He later moved to M-G-M, where he won additional plaudits, and produced several of Judy Garland's pictures: *Presenting Lily Mars, Thousands Cheer, In the Good Old Summertime* and *Summer Stock*. Some of his other well-known productions include *Destry Rides Again, The Great Caruso* and *Love Me or Leave Me*. Mr. Pasternak has written his autobiography, *Easy the Hard Way*, and a cookbook, *Cooking With Love and Paprika*.

I've made many discoveries in my life. Unfortunately, Judy wasn't one of them. Arthur Freed discovered her. Everybody always gives me great credit for discovering Deanna Durbin. Actually, it was an accident that I discovered Deanna, because I wanted Judy. My casting director called up Metro to see if Judy was available for *Three Smart Girls*. He was told that Metro had an option on both girls but they were keeping Judy and letting Deanna go. They made a big mistake in letting Durbin go.

Also, besides the great singing talent or acting talent, the actor
or actress must have the right director—and at that time,
Henry Koster was the right director for Deanna Durbin, and he
brought out the best in her.

—

Judy and Deanna were different types of singers who produced
different emotions. When I saw Judy, I wanted to dance and
sing with her. When I saw Durbin, I wanted to kiss her and fall
in love with her and just sit back and listen.

For a while, Durbin was a much bigger star than Judy. It took
a long time for Judy to capture the world market. Durbin captured
the whole world immediately. The European and South American
countries loved her singing much better than Judy's, because
Judy was typically American.

—

Deanna was not a topic of sensation—except for her talent.
About Judy there are legends—she always made news. People wanted
to write and talk about Judy because she was explosive and
unpredictable.

—

We all make mistakes, but we're not important enough to be
pointed at. I'm sure every young girl went through emotional
situations like they [Deanna and Judy] did but nobody prints this—
the public's not interested in it.

—

You'd have to be a psychiatrist to judge why one child adjusts

A scene from Presenting Lily Mars, *one of the four Judy
Garland films produced by Joe Pasternak*

better than another. Durbin was much more settled. She came from a much happier home life and upbringing and her personal life never created a hullaballoo. She retired early. She knew when to quit—before they quit her. She settled for what life had to offer her. She's still the same delightful girl she ever was.

———

When I met Judy at Metro she said, "Oh my God, this is the man who discovered Deanna Durbin." And I said, "I tried to discover you, but you were not available."

Every picture I made with Judy was an event, because I discovered more and more of her talent and her shortcomings.

———

With Judy it was more difficult to take success than failure. Just imagine—she was fifteen or sixteen years old, and the whole world knew her and loved her.

You know she was in school with Lana Turner and all those glamorous girls, and she sort of felt like she was a little homely girl compared to them. One day Lana turned to her and said, "You know, I'd give all the beauty I have for your talent—the expression in your face—your singing."

———

As a singer-actress-comedienne, she was the most talented person— she could make you laugh and cry at the same time. Of course, her biggest complex was that at times she was a little overweight.

———

At a party, you didn't have to ask her to sing. Whether there are fifteen guests at a party or she's singing at the Palladium, she gives her all.

———

I've never in my life seen an audience pull for a singer like they pull for Judy.

———

She wasn't a solitary person. She loved company. I'm still wondering what happened to her—where things went wrong in her career.

———

Sometimes there was friction between her and the other actors because she was late. I could understand. But they couldn't. It's like a family of five or six children where one is the most talented and it's difficult to hold back your admiration and give everybody the same amount of love.

———

You couldn't stay angry with her very long. She'd come in after doing some foolish things that she couldn't help doing and look at you with those sad, beautiful eyes and start singing and you'd forget you wanted to bawl her out.

———

I've made 105 pictures, only four of them with Judy. But I never ceased to wonder how God had given so much talent to one little person!

JUDY: *The Films*

With Deanna Durbin

Every Sunday (1936)

M-G-M first utilized fourteen-year-old Judy Garland's talents in this two-reel short subject, teaming her with another teenager under contract, Deanna Durbin. Felix Feist was the director of this mini-film, in which Deanna sang "classical" while Judy belted "swing."

With unidentified player, Deanna Durbin, and Sid Silvers

Both youngsters were destined for top stardom, although Durbin was dropped by M-G-M and picked up by Universal, where she enjoyed almost immediate success.

There is some question as to the original title of this short. Joe Pasternak remembers it as *One Sunday Afternoon*, and other sources refer to it as *Every Sunday Afternoon*. Current official M-G-M records list it as *Every Sunday*. (Full-length feature films with the titles *One Sunday Afternoon* and *Every Sunday Afternoon* were subsequently released.)

ARTHUR FREED *comments*: When Deanna Durbin's option was dropped at Metro after this short, Judy was dropped at the

With Deanna Durbin

same time. Except that I ran into Mr. Mayer and saw that they didn't drop Judy.

JOE PASTERNAK *comments:* I couldn't get over how those two little girls—Deanna Durbin and Judy Garland—could belt out songs with such big voices from such little chests and bodies. Usually, strong singers are big-chested.

The role in *Three Smart Girls* [the film Mr. Pasternak produced for Universal which made Deanna Durbin an international star] was originally written for a "hot" or "swing" singer. We saw the short which Judy and Deanna made for M-G-M, and wanted Judy for the part, but she wasn't available—Metro wouldn't let her go. We rewrote the script to suit a classical singer, and got Deanna Durbin.

Pigskin Parade

A 20th Century-Fox Picture (1936)

*Produced by Darryl F. Zanuck
Directed by David Butler
Screenplay by Harry Tugend, Jack Yellan, William Conselman
Based on a story by Art Sheekman, Nat Perrin and Mark Kelly
Music and Lyrics by Lew Pollack, Sidney Mitchell and
    The Yacht Club Boys
Cameraman: Arthur Miller
Editor: Irene Morra*

CAST
*Patsy Kelly, Jack Haley, The Yacht Club Boys, Stuart Erwin,
John Downs, Betty Grable, Arline Judge, Dixie Dunbar,
Judy Garland, Anthony Martin, Fred Kohler, Jr., Grady Sutton,
Elisha Cook, Jr., Eddie Nugent, Julius Tannen, Pat Flaherty,
Si Jenks.*

COMMENTS
Pigskin Parade was Judy's only loan-out during her long association
with M-G-M. It followed the "college football" formula plot
popular at that time, and also featured a Fox contract player named

With Stuart Erwin

With Betty Grable, unidentified player, Johnny Downs, and
Dixie Dunbar

Betty Grable. Reviewers noticed Judy in the film, but it did not particularly advance her career.

What the critics said about
PIGSKIN PARADE

The New York Times

  Also in the newcomer category is Judy Garland, about twelve or thirteen now, about whom the West Coast has been enthusing as a vocal find. . . . She's cute, not too pretty, but a pleasingly fetching personality, who certainly knows how to sell a pop.

Newsweek

A gleeful hybrid of the seasonal football picture and the ubiquitous campus musical comedy. By mistake a jerkwater team is invited north to play Yale. Stu Erwin (hero), Jack Haley and Patsy Kelly (coaches) are three reasons why there is more horseplay than football. The Yacht Club Boys and a lively cast take good care of the singing and dancing.

With Patsy Kelly, Johnny Downs, and Betty Grable

With Sophie Tucker and boarders

Broadway Melody of 1938

A Metro-Goldwyn-Mayer Picture (1937)

Produced by Jack Cummings
Directed by Roy Del Ruth
Screenplay by Jack McGowan
Story by Jack McGowan and Sid Silvers
Music and Lyrics by Nacio Herb Brown and Arthur Freed
Music Director: George Stoll
Music Arrangements: Roger Edens
Dance ensembles by Dave Gould
Cameraman: William Daniels
Editor: Blanche Sewell
Art Director: Cedric Gibbons

CAST
Robert Taylor, Eleanor Powell, George Murphy, Binnie Barnes,
Buddy Ebsen, Sophie Tucker, Judy Garland, Charles Igor Gorin,
Raymond Walburn, Robert Benchley, Willie Howard,
Charles Grapewin, Robert Wildhack, Billy Gilbert, Barnett Parker,
Helen Troy.

With Sophie Tucker

COMMENTS

"Dear Mr. Gable, You Made Me Love You," sang Judy to a photograph of Clark Gable, and the public loved Judy. The fifteen-year-old now had public identification.

Broadway Melody of 1938 was a continuation of the "Broadway Melody" series of musical films that were big hits for M-G-M in the 1930's. The series began with the Academy Award-winning

With Sophie Tucker and Barnett Parker

With chorus

The studio used the "Broadway Melody" series to introduce and develop new talent. Box-office success was insured by peopling the films with the big-name stars under studio contract. This type of picture was popular in the 1930's, as evidenced by Warner Brothers' similar series, "The Gold Diggers of . . ." and Paramount's "The Big Broadcast of . . .", while 20th Century-Fox had "George White's Scandals of . . ."

Broadway Melody of 1938, released in 1937, was a hit, but stardom was still a couple of years off for Judy, while her first co-star, Deanna Durbin, had already achieved international fame.

GEORGE MURPHY *comments:* I recall that when I first saw Judy on the Metro-Goldwyn-Mayer lot, we went into Eleanor Powell's rehearsal bungalow, and Judy and I learned a little chorus of a soft-shoe dance which we did for some of the bosses and which I have bragged about for many years. Working with her on *Broadway Melody* and watching her doing a number with Buddy Ebsen was an unforgettable experience, and it was obvious to all that with all of her charm and childish manners and ways, she apparently was born with a full complement of the finest talents, and as time went on these talents were developed to a greater and greater degree by all the people that the studio could provide, like the great Roger Edens, and the finest dance directors.

With Buddy Ebsen

What the critics said about
BROADWAY MELODY OF 1938

The New York Times
[There are] individual successes in the film . . . [The] amazing
precocity of Judy Garland, Metro's answer to Deanna Durbin. . . .
Miss Garland particularly has a long tour de force in which she
addresses lyrical apostrophes to a picture of Clark Gable. The idea
and words are almost painfully silly—yet Judy . . . puts it over—
in fact with a bang. (BOSLEY CROWTHER)

The New York Herald Tribune
. . . A girl named Judy Garland . . . does a heart-rending song about
her unrequited love for Clark Gable, which the audience seemed
to like. The tunes are crisp and catchy and the final scene, all in
modernistic style, is as original and handsome a setting as the screen
has created. (MARGUERITE TAZELAAR)

Thoroughbreds Don't Cry

A Metro-Goldwyn-Mayer Picture (1937)

Produced by Harry Rapf
Directed by Alfred E. Green
Screenplay by Lawrence Hazard
Story by Eleanore Griffin and J. Walter Ruben
Music and Lyrics by Nacio Herb Brown and Arthur Freed
Editor: Elmo Vernon
Cameraman: Leonard Smith

*With Robert Sinclair and
Mickey Rooney*

CAST
*Judy Garland, Mickey Rooney, Sophie Tucker, C. Aubrey Smith,
Robert Sinclair, Forrester Harvey, Charles D. Brown, Frankie Darro,
Henry Kolker, Helen Troy.*

COMMENTS
This was a racing yarn about Mickey Rooney and Robert Sinclair
trying to train a horse. Garland's vivacious, perky youthful zing
was tossed in to advantage. This marked her first screen appearance
with Mickey Rooney.

What the critics said about
THOROUGHBREDS DON'T CRY

The New York Times
. . . Short on logic but long on pep, it gallops gayly into the stretch. . . .
. . . Mr. Rooney, as the jock, manages to streak with a brilliant

With Sophie Tucker

With Mickey Rooney

performance which lends a certain quality to the whole picture.

Robert Sinclair . . . handles the role of Roger with a sturdy "little manliness" which uncomfortably suggests Freddie Bartholomew, for whom the role was originally intended. Judy Garland is the puppy-love interest who tosses off some scorchy rhythm-singing . . .

Mark this one on your card as all right. (BOSLEY CROWTHER)

The New York Herald Tribune

An appealing picture, especially for children. The story has to do with a racetrack. Mickey is a vain young jockey who has never lost a race and Ronald (Sinclair) is the son of a titled Englishman

With Mickey Rooney and Robert Sinclair

*With Robert Sinclair and
Mickey Rooney*

(C. Aubrey Smith) who has brought his horse to America not only to recoup his waning fortunes but because of his genuine love and belief in Pukka, his horse.

The introduction of the two boys by Judy Garland, who is the niece of the keeper (Sophie Tucker) of the boarding house where Mickey and the other jockeys live is especially enlivening. All except Judy make fun of his English speech and gentlemanly manners. . . .

Miss Garland does several imitations nicely. . . . Miss Tucker, in a rather small role, plays it with sympathy and not too much emphasis.

Mickey Rooney gives a really fine performance . . . and Robert Sinclair is genuinely appealing. (MARGUERITE TAZELAAR)

Newsweek
Three child actors, Judy Garland, Mickey Rooney, and Robert Sinclair, handle the occasional laughs and thrills of this frankly hokum story of an English sportsman who brings a race horse and grandson to the American tracks.

With Lynne Carver, Allan Jones, and Reginald Gardiner

Everybody Sing

A Metro-Goldwyn-Mayer Picture (1938)

Produced by Harry Rapf
Directed by Edwin L. Marin
Screenplay by Florence Ryerson and Edgar Allan Woolf
Additional dialogue by James Gruen
Musical interpolations and vocal arrangements by Roger Edens
Music and Lyrics by Bronislau Kaper and Walter Jurmann,
    Gus Kahn, Bert Kalmar and Harry Ruby
Musical Director: Dr. William Axt
Cameraman: Joseph Ruttenberg

With schoolmates

With Fanny Brice, Henry Armetta, and Allan Jones

CAST

Allan Jones, Judy Garland, Fanny Brice, Reginald Owen, Billie Burke, Reginald Gardiner, Lynne Carver, Helen Troy, Monty Woolley, Adia Kuznetzoff, Henry Armetta, Michelette Burani, Mary Forbes.

COMMENTS

Garland by now was becoming a personality. The song "You Made Me Love You" had swept the country, and "Everybody Sing" gave her the opportunity to sing "swing" and play opposite the seasoned performers Fanny Brice, Allan Jones and Billie Burke.

With Andrew Toombes and Fanny Brice

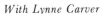

Judy, being promoted by M-G-M, received second billing to Allan Jones. Fanny Brice, an enormous success on Broadway and on radio, never achieved star stature in films. Fanny received third billing in this film, in which she played the maid of a wealthy family with two daughters. Lynne Carver played the older daughter, and Judy was her younger sister.

What the critics said about
EVERYBODY SING

The New York Times
Several things, all more or less negative in character, are wrong about *Everybody Sing,* at the Capitol, but the chief trouble is that everybody sings—not merely Allan Jones and Judy Garland, whom we expected and were prepared for—but a rousing Pilgrim's Chorus composed of the whole darn cast of characters. There are scenes in drawing rooms, in bedrooms, in theatres, in night clubs, in a Chinatown bus, and they are all singing scenes. It is necessary to be awfully fair-minded and detached in order not to come away from *Everybody Sing* filled with a positive hatred of the human larynx.

It is, of course, only fair to admit that Judy Garland of the rhythm, writin' and 'rithmetic age is a superb vocal technician, despite her not exactly underemphasized immaturity, and that Allan Jones sings with a microphonic goldenness which occasionally almost leads you to forget the words and music. But the point is, they do sing, and it just isn't desirable to sing so often. Even in the hare-brained context provided by Fanny Brice, Reginald Owen, Billie Burke and Reginald Gardiner (who used to do imitations of wallpaper), it seems a little queer.

The burden of our lament, though, is for the misuse of

Fanny Brice, who is now being advertised—to your Broadway and hers—as "the Baby Snooks of radio." Nobody has any right to try and foist upon us a cut Brice, robbed of those incomparably subtle touches of vulgarity for which Fanny is noted and widely beloved. As a Russian servant in a mad household of stage people whose waning fortunes are retrieved by Judy (that's the whole story), she sometimes manages, by sheer, irrepressible genius, to be funny, but never Fanny. And it's Fanny we care about. (B.R.C.)

Time
Everybody Sing stars fifteen-year-old Judy Garland, Hollywood's latest child singer. She turns the morning singing hour of the Colvin School for Girls into a swing session. Sent home to the jittery bosom of a family infected with the slightly threadbare lunacy which has been bothering recent cinema families, she croons her way to a career with the help of Olga, a screwball maid (Fanny Brice), and Ricky (Allan Jones), a singing chef.

With Freddie Bartholomew

Listen, Darling

A Metro-Goldwyn-Mayer Picture (1938)

Produced by Jack Cummings
Directed by Edwin L. Marin
Screenplay by Elaine Ryan and Anne Morrison Chapin
Based on a story by Katherine Brush
Music and Lyrics by Al Hoffman, Al Lewis and Murray Mencher;
  Joseph McCarthy, Milton Ager and James F. Henley
Musical arrangements: Roger Edens
Musical Director: George Stoll
Cameraman: Charles Lawton, Jr.
Editor: Blanche Sewell
Art Director: Cedric Gibbons

With Freddie Bartholomew, Scotty
Beckett, and Mary Astor

[59]

With Freddie Bartholomew and Charles Grapewin

With Charles Grapewin and Freddie Bartholomew

CAST
Freddie Bartholomew, Judy Garland, Mary Astor, Walter Pidgeon, Alan Hale, Scotty Beckett, Barnett Parker, Gene Lockhart, Charley Grapewin.

COMMENTS

Judy was given the chance to demonstrate more acting ability in this yarn about youngsters trying to get their widowed mother matched with the right mate. She also sang two songs: "Zing Went the Strings of My Heart" and "Nobody's Baby."

Mary Astor played her widowed mother, Freddie Bartholomew her friend, and Scotty Beckett her brother. The kids, along with kindly and humorous Charley Grapewin, managed to steer their mother from "wrong man" Gene Lockhart into the arms of "right man" Walter Pidgeon.

Metro was capitalizing on the popularity of their leading child star, Freddie Bartholomew (whose recent successes included *David Copperfield* and *Little Lord Fauntleroy*), and paired him with Judy. Freddie's career was nearing its end, while Judy, Mary Astor, and Walter Pidgeon were to go on to greater heights.

In 1938, the career of Mary Astor, a big star in the silent and early talkie era, was waning and she was playing the role of a mother. It was almost unheard of, in the 1930's, for a glamorous star to admit being over twenty-nine. Indeed, many of them in their late 30's and early 40's were still playing ingénues. However, Mary Astor, like Bette Davis and a few other film stars, was more of an actress and less concerned with her image as a leading lady. She gave a convincing and charming performance. (Six years later she again played Judy's mother in *Meet Me in St. Louis.*)

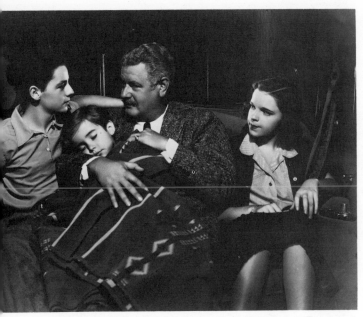

With Freddie Bartholomew, Scotty Beckett, and Alan Hale

With Alan Hale, Freddie Bartholomew, Scotty Beckett, Mary Astor, and Walter Pidgeon

Two years after *Listen, Darling*, Miss Astor scored in *The Maltese Falcon* and then received an Oscar for her supporting role in *The Great Lie*.

Walter Pidgeon, a competent seasoned actor, had not been established as a star by 1938, but in the early 40's he came into his own when M-G-M teamed him with Greer Garson.

Scotty Beckett, too, became popular in movies.

Listen, Darling was a vehicle that served them all. It was a pleasant comedy and another exposure of Judy's talents and demonstration of her abilities to hold her own with pros.

What the critics said about
     LISTEN, DARLING

The New York Times
An extremely pleasant—winsome would be a better word—picture about two youngsters who kidnap a matrimonially eligible widow, lock her in a trailer, and start touring the countryside in search of a suitable husband. . . .

Freddie Bartholomew and Judy Garland—with little Scotty Beckett's unconscious assistance—conduct their matrimonial tour with charming unworldliness, despite the surface sophistication of their enterprise. . . .

The comedy has been nicely turned out by Mary Astor, Walter Pidgeon, Alan Hale, Gene Lockhart and Charley Grapewin, among the adults, and by all three youngsters. Besides being a charming little miss, Judy Garland has a fresh young voice which she uses happily on "Zing Went the Strings of My Heart," "On a Bumpy Road To Love" and "Ten Pins in the Sky." . . .
It is really a natural, pleasant and sensible little film. . . .
                                    (FRANK NUGENT)

*With Mickey Rooney, Ann Rutherford,
and Lana Turner*

Love Finds Andy Hardy

A Metro-Goldwyn-Mayer-Picture (1938)

*Directed by George B. Seitz
Screenplay by William Indwig
From the stories by Vivien R. Bretherton, based on characters
     created by Aurania Rouverol
Music and Lyrics by Mack Gordon, Harry Revel and Roger Edens
Cameraman: Lester White
Editor: Ben Lewis*

CAST
*Lewis Stone, Mickey Rooney, Judy Garland, Cecilia Parker,
Fay Holden, Ann Rutherford, Betty Ross Clarke, Lana Turner,
Marie Blake, Don Castle, Gene Reynolds, Mary Howard,
George Breakston, Raymond Hatton.*

With Don Castle and Mickey Rooney

With Mickey Rooney

COMMENTS

The Andy Hardy films were already a big success. To advance
Judy's career, M-G-M decided to introduce a new character into
the series, Betsy Booth. She, like every other girl in the mythical
town of Carvel, fell head over heels in love with Andy Hardy,
in the person of Mickey Rooney. Ann Rutherford and a new young
redhead under contract to M-G-M, Lana Turner, were also
featured in this film.

The first Andy Hardy picture was *A Family Affair* (1937),
which starred Lionel Barrymore as Judge Hardy, Spring Byington
as Mrs. Hardy and Mickey Rooney as young Andy. The film and
Mickey were so well received that a series of pictures followed.
Barrymore was replaced by Lewis Stone and Spring Byington by
Fay Holden. For the remainder of the series the cast remained
intact—Lewis Stone, Fay Holden, Cecilia Parker as Andy's sister,
Sara Haden as his aunt and Ann Rutherford as his girl Polly.

Along with Judy Garland, Lana Turner, and Ann Rutherford,
many screen newcomers were introduced or developed through the
Hardy series, including Kathryn Grayson, Esther Williams and
Ray MacDonald.

What the critics said about
    LOVE FINDS ANDY HARDY

The New York Times
Our favorite neighbors, the Hardys, are visiting again, this time in a
felicitous little comedy which goes, and goes delightfully . . .

With Lana Turner and
Mickey Rooney

under the name *Love Finds Andy Hardy*. The best of it is that love not only finds Andy Hardy but finds him being played by Mickey Rooney . . . he's the perfect composite of everybody's kid brother.

If you must know what happens we will report it simply that the Hardys, severally and collectively, are up to their old crises again. There is the crisis of the new cook. There is the crisis of Marion's attempt at coffee-making. There is the crisis of Andy's car— a $12 down payment and $8 to go. There is the crisis of grandmother's stroke. There is the crisis of the Christmas Eve dance. . . .

. . . The nicest thing about all the Hardy crises, they resolve themselves so beautifully.

. . . a friendly, likeable show. (FRANK NUGENT)

With Cecilia Parker, Lewis Stone,
Fay Holden, and Mickey Rooney

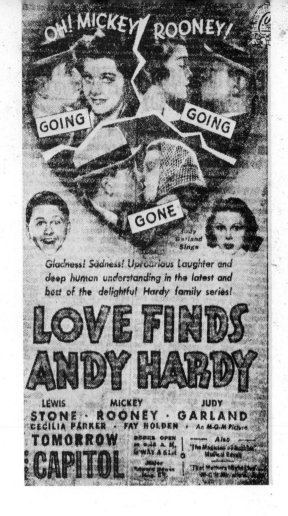

The New York Herald Tribune

Altogether the best of the "Judge Hardy" series . . . Mickey Rooney
gives an exuberant performance. . . . If the comedy falters, it is
because an ill-advised attempt has been made to bring in some
musical numbers in the ending. Judy Garland sings them and they
are catchy enough pieces but they have no proper place in this
sort of show. Miss Garland is the least effective of the young players
who have a hand in the photoplay. Ann Rutherford and
Lana Turner are far better. . . . They have a bit too much glamour
for youngsters, but they prove good foils for Mickey Rooney's
capers. (HOWARD BARNES)

Time

Fourth item in M-G-M's lively series on the homely, 100%
American problems of the Hardy family, Love Finds Andy Hardy
rises above the standard not only of its predecessors, but also of
most of its producer's most expensive features. . . .

   Such cinema families as the Hardys and Twentieth Century-Fox's
Joneses are well on their way to developing for modern
cinemaddicts the kind of cumulative box-office appeal once exercised
by old-time serials.

The Wizard of Oz

A Metro-Goldwyn-Mayer Picture (1939)

Produced by Mervyn LeRoy
Directed by Victor Fleming
Screenplay by Noel Langley, Florence Ryerson and
*   Edgar Allan Woolf*
Adapted from the book by L. Frank Baum
Musical adaptation by Herbert Stothart
Lyrics by E. Y. Harburg
Music by Harold Arlen
Special effects: Arnold Gillespie
Musical numbers: Bobby Connolly
Cameraman: Harold Rosson
Editor: Blanche Sewell

CAST
Judy Garland, Frank Morgan, Ray Bolger, Bert Lahr, Jack Haley,
Billie Burke, Margaret Hamilton, Charles Grapewin, Clara Blondick,
Pat Walshe, The Singer Midgets as the Munchkins, and Toto.

COMMENTS
A milestone in Judy Garland's career. Each year, this film

With Clara Blondick, Margaret Hamilton, and Charles Grapewin

enchants new generations of moviegoers and continues to charm those who return again and again to the land of Oz.

One of the most ideally cast movies in the history of the cinema, *The Wizard of Oz* remains to this day a classic in all respects. (Victor Fleming, the director, was called from this film to complete direction of *Gone With the Wind*.)

Judy was seventeen years old when the film was released in August, 1939. She won a special Academy Award for "The Best Juvenile Performance of the Year."

In the film Judy introduced the Arlen-Harburg song, "Over the Rainbow," a song to this day synonymous with Judy Garland.

The Wizard of Oz was one of the biggest budgeted pictures of the time, with photography in both black and white and color. Metro-Goldwyn-Mayer spared no expense in creating the magical land of Oz.

With Margaret Hamilton (as the Wicked Witch of the West) and Ray Bolger (as the Scarecrow)

[67]

With Jack Haley (as the Tin Woodman) and Ray Bolger

Oz was populated by the tiny Munchkins (The Singer Midgets), the Straw Man (Ray Bolger), the Tin Woodman (Jack Haley), the Cowardly Lion (Bert Lahr), Good Witch Glinda (Billie Burke), the Wicked Witch of the West (Margaret Hamilton), and, of course, by the fast-talking Wizard of Oz (Frank Morgan).

The Wizard will grant their requests (Dorothy—Judy Garland—

With Ray Bolger and Jack Haley

With Bert Lahr (as the Cowardly Lion), Jack Haley, Ray Bolger, and Margaret Hamilton

wants to return to Kansas; the Straw Man yearns for a brain; the Tin Woodman longs for a heart; and the Cowardly Lion seeks courage) only after they overcome the evils of the Wicked Witch of the West.

In their adventures Dorothy's three friends gradually learn that they possess within themselves the qualities they were asking for. And Dorothy, by believing, has all along possessed the ability to return to her home and family.

An incredibly timeless script preserved the spirit of the book, and the theme and presentation of the film make it not only a delight for children but an experience for adults. The marriage of

With the Singer Midgets (as the Munchkins)

*With Bert Lahr, Ray Bolger, and
Jack Haley*

the role of Dorothy and the talents of Judy Garland catapulted
the youngster to the heights of film stardom and for the first time
made her an internationally known personality.

Many people still think of Judy Garland as little Dorothy in
The Wizard of Oz.

ARTHUR FREED *comments:* Before I was a producer, Mr. Mayer
had spoken to me about producing pictures, so I bought
The Wizard of Oz from Sam Goldwyn. He had owned it for
years and never made it. I started out being the associate producer
of the film, but it was an expensive picture and Mr. Mayer
suggested I take Mervyn LeRoy to produce it. Both Mervyn and I

*With Bert Lahr, Ray Bolger, and
Jack Haley*

With Billie Burke (as the Good Witch Glinda)

wanted Judy for the role of Dorothy, but the front office wanted
to play it safe and said, "Let's borrow Shirley Temple."
They couldn't borrow her, thank God! At least not for that
particular picture.

I brought Harold Arlen and "Yip" Harburg out to write the
score. "Over the Rainbow" was taken out of the film after a
preview, but I had it put back in before the picture was released.

What the critics said about
THE WIZARD OF OZ

The New York Times
A delightful piece of wonder-working which had the youngsters'
eyes shining and brought a quietly amused gleam to the wiser
ones of the oldsters. Judy Garland's Dorothy is a pert and fresh-
faced miss with the wonder-lit eyes of a believer in fairy tales.
(FRANK S. NUGENT)

The New York Daily News
4 stars. Judy Garland is perfectly cast as Dorothy. She is as clever a
little actress as she is a singer and her special style of vocalizing
is ideally adapted to the music of the picture (KATE CAMERON)

The New York Post
Excellent. Brilliantly Technicolored . . . a beautiful and humorous
fantasy the appeal of which is not limited to juvenile trade.
The performances are beyond cavil. Miss Garland makes a delightful
Dorothy. [It's] a picture to put on your things-to-do today list.
(ARCHER WINSTEN)

With Jack Haley, Ray Bolger, Frank Morgan (as the Wizard), and Bert Lahr

The New York Herald Tribune
Judy Garland makes a delightful Dorothy as she wanders through Oz until she realizes that all the wonderment in the world can be had in her own back yard. . . . *The Wizard of Oz* is an amusing and spectacular film. . . .

Time
. . . No children's tale is Hollywood's *Wizard of Oz*. Lavish in sets, adult in humor, it is a Broadway spectacular translated into make-believe. . . . Its tornado rivals Sam Goldwyn's *The Hurricane*. Its final sequence is as sentimental as *Little Women*. . . .

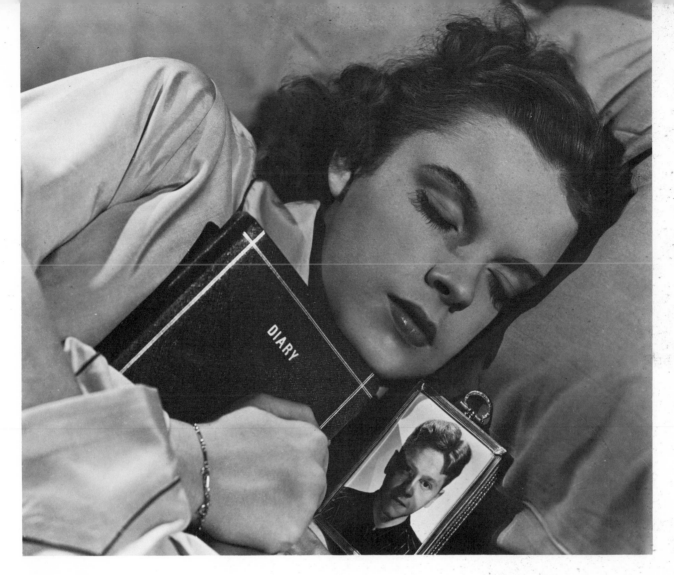

Babes in Arms

A Metro-Goldwyn-Mayer Picture (1939)

Produced by Arthur Freed
Directed by Busby Berkeley
Screenplay by Jack McGowan and Kay Van Riper
Based on a play by Richard Rodgers and Lorenz Hart
Music by Rodgers and Hart, Nacio Herb Brown and Arthur Freed,
*   Harold Arlen and E. Y. Harburg*
Orchestral arrangements by Leo Arnaud and George Bassman
Cameraman: Ray June
Editor: Frank Sullivan
Art Director: Cedric Gibbons

CAST
Mickey Rooney, Judy Garland, Charles Winninger, Guy Kibbee,
June Preisser, Grace Hoyes, Betty Jaynes, Douglas MacPhail,
Rand Brooks, Leni Lynn, John Sheffield, Henry Hull, Barnett Parker,
Ann Shoemaker, Margaret Hamilton, Joseph Crebon,
George McKay, Henry Roquemore, Lelah Tyler.

With Mickey Rooney

COMMENTS

In this film, Judy and Mickey Rooney displayed their multi-faceted talents and utilized all their background and experience from vaudeville.

It was a delightful tale of show business folk, showcasing these two most popular youngsters of the day.

Their youth and charm and vigor seemed infectious. Reviewers agreed.

ARTHUR FREED *comments:* The first time Judy starred for me was in *Babes in Arms,* with Mickey Rooney, who was the biggest star at the studio at that time. It was the biggest Metro picture of the year. The picture cost about $600,000 to produce, and grossed over two million dollars in the U.S. alone.

What the critics said about
    BABES IN ARMS

The New York Times
Babes in Arms—to express it in two words—is Mickey Rooney. . . . Because of his precocious virtuosity, Master Rooney is entitled to be picketed by Judy Garland, who does a beautiful imitation of Mrs. Roosevelt's broadcasting manner and has to sing another song to a photograph besides. . . . If we must have hokum, let us at least disguise it gracefully, even when it's with music.

With Mickey Rooney

With Mickey Rooney

Portraying Eleanor Roosevelt to Mickey Rooney's Franklin D. Douglas MacPhail on steps.

With Mickey Rooney

The New York Post
. . . a brightly entertaining screen version of the Rodgers and Hart legit musical. Perked up by . . . Mickey's mugging and undeniable song and dance talents, and by Judy Garland's simply swell sense of swing . . . *Babes in Arms* is quite a show. It moves fast, with guaranteed laughs and lots of sure-fire tunes. (IRENE THIRER)

The New York Daily News
The irresistible team of Mickey Rooney and Judy Garland are currently displaying their varied talents from the Capitol screen in *Babes in Arms*. As an entertainment it has lost some of its original sophistication and the elastic snap with which it went over on

the stage. But it has gained in comic interludes and serves to introduce
several new screen personalities. Mickey performs with all the
youthful vigor he is capable of throwing into a screen role.

The New York Herald Tribune
Mickey and Judy better than ever. (ROBERT DANA)

Andy Hardy Meets Debutante

A Metro-Goldwyn-Mayer Picture (1940)

Directed by George B. Seitz
Screenplay by Annalee Whitmore and Thomas Seller,
*   based on characters created by Aurania Rouverol*
Cameramen: Sidney Wagner, Charles Lawton
Editor: Harold F. Kress

CAST

Lewis Stone, Mickey Rooney, Cecilia Parker, Fay Holden,
Judy Garland, Ann Rutherford, Diana Lewis, George Breakston,
Sara Haden, Addison Richard, George Lessey, Gladys Blake,
Cy Kendall, Clyde Willson.

COMMENTS
Judy and Mickey were back in Carvel.

What the critics said about
    ANDY HARDY MEETS DEBUTANTE

The New York Times
Now that all good Americans have taken to talking and thinking a
lot about democracy, it was to be expected that Metro's Hardy
family would get around to the subject too. . . .

*With Mickey Rooney, Cecilia Parker,
Lewis Stone, Fay Holden, and Sara
Haden*

The subject, you see, comes up in connection with Andy's
thwarted pursuit of America's No. 1 "deb" during a visit to
New York; and the gleaming evidence of social equality in this great
land of ours is revealed to the frivolous youth who was on the
verge of becoming a horrid snob, when his daddy, the good old
judge, won a case in the big New York courts. Thereby democracy

With Mickey Rooney

With Mickey Rooney

is proved, Andy, and all of us too, infer that "debs" are mere folks like anyone else.

. . . But don't worry, this little digression into social philosophy doesn't seriously encroach upon the interest uppermost in Andy's mind, which is young ladies. . . .

. . . Just another milestone in this popular family series, a milestone to be welcomed, that is. But we can't help speculating upon how much they all look alike. (BOSLEY CROWTHER)

The New York Herald Tribune
. . . The photoplay is certainly not one of the best Hardy shows. It has the famous family descending on New York, where the judge wins a case against high-pressure corporation lawyers who are trying to close an orphanage, and Andy breaks into high society. . . .

Three leading women have been enlisted for the offering. They are adequate enough foils for the Rooney antics but they rarely get inside their impersonations. Judy Garland is altogether the best of them, playing a hero-worshiping girl from the city who has the small-town boy invited to a coming out party and attracts his romantic interest momentarily by singing some torch songs. . . . (HOWARD BARNES)

Time
Andy Hardy Meets Debutante marks Mickey Rooney's ninth appearance as bratty Andy Hardy. . . .

As such oldsters as Wallace Beery, Lionel Barrymore, and Lewis Stone have discovered, Mickey Rooney thrives on his ability and determination to steal anything up to a death scene from a colleague. Some of Cinemactor Stone's heartiest chuckles may be explained by the fact that seventeen-year-old Judy Garland, growing prettier by the picture and armed for this one with two good songs, "Alone" and "I'm Nobody's Baby," treats Mickey with a dose of his own medicine.

Strike Up the Band

A Metro-Goldwyn-Mayer Picture (1940)

Produced by Arthur Freed
Directed by Busby Berkeley
Screenplay by John Monks, Jr., and Fred Finklehoffe
Lyrics and Music by Roger Edens, George and Ira Gershwin,
*   and Arthur Freed*
Musical Director: George Stoll
Cameraman: Ray June
Editor: Ben Lewis

With June Preisser

[81]

*With Francis Pierlot and
Mickey Rooney*

CAST
*Mickey Rooney, Judy Garland, Paul Whiteman, June Preisser,
William Tracy, Larry Nunn, Margaret Early, Ann Shoemaker,
Francis Pierlot, Virginia Brissac, George Lessey, Enid Bennett,
Howard Hickman, Sarah Edwards, Milton Kibbee,
Helen Jerome Eddy.*

COMMENTS
Strike Up the Band was a campus musical, spotlighting
Mickey Rooney as a drum-playing kid trying to join Paul Whiteman's
orchestra, with the help of girl friend Judy Garland.

   Both Mickey and Judy had an amazingly contemporary quality
which came through in this and all of their other films. Even
when viewed today the films may seem dated, but Garland
and Rooney don't.

What the critics said about
    STRIKE UP THE BAND

The New York Times
Roll out the red carpet, folks, and stand by. That boy is here

With Mickey Rooney and Larry Nunn

With Larry Nunn, Mickey Rooney,
and William Tracy

again, the Pied Piper of the box offices, the eighth or ninth wonder
of the world, the kid himself—in short, Mickey Rooney. With a
capable assist by Judy Garland, Mr. Rooney strutted into the
Capitol on Saturday at the head of *Strike Up the Band,* and it should
surprise no one this morning to learn that the show is his from
beginning to end.

   . . . As they say in Hollywood, this show has everything—music,
laughter, tears, etc., etc. As usual, everything is a little too much.

   . . . But in the sketches and musical numbers the film goes into
high gear and Mr. Rooney et al. are at the top of their form.
Call him cocky and brash, but he has the sort of exuberant talent
that keeps your eyes on the screen, whether he's banging the
trap-drums, prancing through a Conga, or hamming the old ham
actors. The music is rollicking, especially "Strike Up the Band,"
and "La Conga," sung with a good deal of animal spirits by
Miss Garland.

   . . . *Strike Up the Band* is spanking good entertainment. (T.S.)

The New York Herald Tribune
Following the general pattern of *Babes in Arms,* Mickey Rooney
and Judy Garland romp through another boisterous screen musical
in *Strike Up the Band.* The title and the title song have been
lifted from the Gershwin-Kaufman show . . . but otherwise . . . the
offering bears no resemblance to its stage namesake. Instead of a
satirical war continuity it offers a series of jam sessions. Instead of
Clark and McCullough it presents Rooney and Garland getting
well into the groove for Metro-Goldwyn-Mayer. The important
point is that the juvenile stars give the show all the punch of a
sure-fire hit.

With Mickey Rooney

. . . Garland is soulful and full of song. . . . When it is good, *Strike Up the Band* is extremely entertaining. Busby Berkeley has staged it with a strong accent on swing music, relating a tale of high school youngsters who syncopate and sing their way into national prominence.

If you have ever seen Mickey Rooney there is little point in hearing about his latest performance. He is just as effective and just as hammy as he ever was. . . .

Miss Garland plays her part in the proceedings with considerable more integrity and sings the various songs, from "Our Love Affair," "Strike Up the Band" and "My Wonderful One" to "Drummer Boy," with a vitality that conceals her lack of musicianship. . . .

Newsweek

When Metro-Goldwyn-Mayer channeled the bounce and brashness of Mickey Rooney, Judy Garland, and a castful of precocious youngsters into a musical called *Babes in Arms* last year, coins clinked in box offices throughout the land. *Strike Up the Band,* a second try in that exuberant groove, lacks the first film's spontaneity and zip, but should come close to matching its popularity.

. . . Undismayed in the face of such comprehensive competition [Mickey Rooney], Judy Garland does some monopolizing of her own with a score that includes a possible new hit ("Our Love Affair"), a parody, and a handful of dated favorites.

Little Nelly Kelly

A Metro-Goldwyn-Mayer Picture (1940)

Produced by Arthur Freed
Directed by Norman Taurog
Screenplay by Jack McGowan
Based on the musical comedy by George M. Cohan
Cameraman: Ray June
Editor: Frederick Y. Smith

CAST
Judy Garland, George Murphy, Charles Winninger,
Douglas MacPhail, Arthur Shields, Rita Page, Forrester Harvey.

COMMENTS
Judy was allowed to grow up in this film, which provided her
with her most difficult dramatic assignment up to that point.
The story concerned a young girl in Ireland (Judy Garland) who
married the man she loved (George Murphy) against the wishes
of her father (Charles Winninger).

She played a dual role, first as George Murphy's wife who dies
in childbirth, and later as Murphy's young daughter. She handled

the death scene with sensitive skill and conveyed two totally different and believable characterizations.

Judy was proving her ability to make the transition from juvenile to adult roles.

Many of her juvenile contemporaries were not as successful in making this adjustment.

GEORGE MURPHY *comments: Little Nelly Kelly* has always been one of my favorite pictures. I recall playing a scene with Judy in *Little Nelly Kelly* which was in the hospital when she was about to die during the birth of her only child, and I assure one and all that this was one of the greatest dramatic scenes that I

With Charles Winninger, George Murphy, and Douglas MacPhail

With George Murphy and Charles Winninger

have ever witnessed. It took me longer to get over the scene than it took Judy. And you might be interested that when the scene was finished the complete set was empty, with the exception of Norman Taurog, the director, Judy, and myself. The grips, electricians, carpenters and all these so-called hard-bitten workers around the set were so emotionally affected that they all had to get off the set so that their sobs would not disturb or disrupt the sound track.

ARTHUR FREED *comments:* I had seen *Little Nelly Kelly* as a kid, when George Cohan had done it on Broadway. Cohan wouldn't sell anything to pictures. I finally had lunch with him in New York, we got along well, and I wound up buying the play for Judy. We added more songs for the film.

What the critics said about
LITTLE NELLY KELLY

The New York Daily News
2½ stars. . . . Long drawn-out battle of the sexes and an over-sentimental story of an Irishman's love for his daughter and the latter's efforts to escape the parental influence.

Judy Garland in the double role . . . does her best, but even her beguiling exuberance and her sweet way with a ballad cannot entirely overcome the deficiencies of the story.

George Murphy . . . gives a good performance and Charles Winninger . . . remains in character from beginning to end.

(KATE CAMERON)

With George Murphy

*With Charles Winninger, Paul Kelly, Edward Everett Horton,
and Jackie Cooper*

Ziegfeld Girl

A Metro-Goldwyn-Mayer Picture (1941)

Produced by Pandro S. Berman
Directed by Robert Z. Leonard
Screenplay by Marguerite Roberts and Sonya Levien
Based on an original story by William Anthony McGuire
Music and Lyrics by Nacio Herb Brown, Gus Kahn, Roger Edens,
*   Harry Carroll, Joseph McCarthy, Edward Gallagher*
*   and Al Shean*
Cameraman: Ray June
Editor: Blanche Sewell

*With Al Shean and
Charles Winninger*

With Charles Winninger, Paul Kelly,
Al Shean, and Edward Everett Horton

CAST
James Stewart, Judy Garland, Hedy Lamarr, Lana Turner,
Tony Martin, Jackie Cooper, Ian Hunter, Charles Winninger,
Edward Everett Horton, Philip Dorn, Paul Kelly, Eve Arden,
Dan Dailey, Jr., Al Shean, Fay Holden, Felix Bressart,
Rose Hobart.

COMMENTS
Although this movie was a vehicle for Lana Turner, which enabled
her to graduate from starlet to star, Judy was not lost in the
shuffle. Again M-G-M provided her with a part which had qualities
enabling her to display both her musical and dramatic ability in
an adult-juvenile role.

With Charles Winninger

With Hedy Lamarr and Lana Turner

Judy had literally grown up on screen before the public's eye. Her stature as a film star was evident by her billing for this picture. She got second billing to James Stewart and above Hedy Lamarr, although Hedy was at the peak of her fame as a glamour girl.

The violin background music for Judy's scenes was reminiscent of the score of *The Wizard of Oz*. In the movies, if something works, it's used again—and again and again.

What the critics said about
ZIEGFELD GIRL

The New York Herald Tribune
Judy Garland is especially good as a youngster who becomes a star under a strict code of showmanship. . . . (HOWARD BARNES)

The New York Times
Judy Garland, with her head-over-heels excitement, counts for
something. . . .

Time
. . . Miss Garland warbles a torrid, tropical tune, "Minnie from
Trinidad" with true professional gusto. Miss Turner manages the
limbs that are to go into limbo and an occasional dramatic
sequence with talent, and Miss Lamarr does not spare her uncanny
physical charms.
 . . . It cost M-G-M $5,000 to pick the chorus for *Ziegfeld Girl*.
It was worth it. The dozen front-line show girls should paralyze
the most case-hardened stage-door-Johnny . . . Like the Ziegfeld Girls
of old, they do not have to act, just undulate.
 Their undulations take place on the three ornate sets devised by
begoggled Cedric Gibbons. Best of them is the Trinidad set: a
forest of 150-foot bamboo trees clustered with tufted satin starfish
and giant seashells.

Newsweek
. . . Judy Garland sings and dances her way enthusiastically from
tank-town vaudeville to the New Amsterdam Theatre and
Charles Winninger, as her father, turns out to be the Gallagher of
the famous Gallagher and Shean team, while Shean is played
with nostalgic gusto by Al Shean himself. . . .

With Tony Martin

Life Begins for Andy Hardy

A Metro-Goldwyn-Mayer Picture (1941)

Directed by George B. Seitz
Screenplay by Agnes Christine Johnston
Based on characters created by Aurania Rouverol
Music Director: George Stoll
Cameraman: Lester White
Editor: Elmo Vernon
Art Director: Cedric Gibbons

CAST
Lewis Stone, Mickey Rooney, Judy Garland, Fay Holden,
Ann Rutherford, Sara Haden, Patricia Dane, Ray McDonald.

COMMENTS
This was Judy's last visit to Andy Hardy and Carvel. She had
outgrown the series, which continued successfully for several more
years. Although Judy did not appear in any additional Hardy
episodes, she was teamed with Mickey Rooney in other hit films.

M-G-M's Andy Hardy series was both a critical and a financial
success. George Seitz directed the pictures. They were produced
at modest cost, and each film earned tremendous profits.

It is reported that Louis B. Mayer, after seeing one of the

With Mickey Rooney

Hardy films, said: "This is it. Don't make them any better."
He felt that any attempts at improvement would cause the films
to lose their charm and their market.

What the critics said about
LIFE BEGINS FOR ANDY HARDY

The New York Times
The boy grows older and a mite wiser in the ways of the world in
Life Begins for Andy Hardy, though Mickey Rooney plays him with
the same boyish gusto he has exhibited in the past ten episodes
of this popular series.

. . . Andy feels that "today I am a man" and sets off for
New York to make good on his own for a month before deciding
between work and more school. Poor little Betsy Booth, still
mooning over the cruelly unattentive Andy, accompanies him to the
big city and watches over him with all the solicitude of a
mother. . . . Judy Garland's talent is by no means taxed in the
role of Betsy.

. . . *Life Begins for Andy Hardy* is a considerable improvement
over some of the more recent ones, but it could have been
improved. . . .

But if you like the Hardys—and who doesn't—then this one
is your dish. (T.M.P.)

The New York Herald Tribune
Life Begins for Andy Hardy is just another exposition of the lad
who braves the big city for awhile, has his hungry days, learns some
sense by his experiences and returns home ready to follow his
father's suggestions of a college education.

Mickey Rooney, Judy Garland, Lewis Stone and two newcomers,
Patricia Dane and Ray MacDonald, work hard to sustain
the film . . . .

... Judy Garland as the faithful hopeful admirer of the Hardy heir is helpful in both the Carvel and New York settings.

(ROBERT DANA)

Newsweek
GROWN-UP ANDY HARDY RUNS INTO A BIT OF CENSOR TROUBLE.

Four years ago Metro-Goldwyn-Mayer adapted a Broadway play called *Skidding,* presented it under the title *A Family Affair,* and walked into streets paved with gold. The locale, a small town known as Carvel, could have been in Ohio or Indiana; studio chiefs never bothered to pin it to the map. From that first B offering, planned as just another program filler, the saga of Judge Hardy and his family has developed into a moneymaking institution that is expected to attract another sizable fortune to the box office before Mickey Rooney's "Andy Hardy"—who is evidently growing a good deal faster than Mickey Rooney himself—settles down into dull, adult respectability.

Through the first ten installments of the Hardy series, the family's problems were accepted as inspiring, middle-class Americana for man, woman, and child. But while the eleventh chapter, *Life Begins for Andy Hardy,* carries on in the same folksy tradition, something has happened to Andy. As a matter of fact, Andy is eighteen now, out of high school and, as he explains it with the exuberant pride that comes before a fall, "I am a man!" And with Andy's alleged maturity, the National Legion of Decency has decided he is no longer the ideal playmate for less experienced adolescents. As a result, the legion, warning "parents who had

With Mickey Rooney

With unidentified player

come to regard Hardy pictures as appropriate entertainment for children," classified the new film as "unobjectionable for adults."

This decision that will lose Andy a portion of his younger following stems directly from that young man's inability to decide whether or not he wants to go to college and waste "the ten best years of his life" to become a lawyer like his father. Instead, Andy goes to New York for a month to get a job and size up the world. Eventually he does get a job as office boy; he also takes quite a kicking around from the Big, Cruel City before he decides to come home and settle for an education. In the meantime, he has picked up some invaluable information about the Ways of Women as demonstrated by Patricia Dane, a pert and pretty telephone operator with a warm nature.

Ordinarily the legion doesn't explain the reasons behind its picture ratings. Evidently the strange case of the aging Andy Hardy was important enough to require amplification. The legion, specifically, objected to two scenes: In the one Lewis Stone, as the slightly worried judge, gives his dreamy-eyed son a nick-of-time lecture on the importance of fidelity to the girl—she may be in pigtails yet—he will one day marry; in the other the telephone operator, separated from her husband, invites Andy into her apartment for an evening of unspecified "fun." Needless to say, Carvel's leading citizen survives this trying experience none the worse for wearing his heart on his sleeve and perhaps a little more tolerant of the motherly attentions of his sincerest admirer, Judy Garland.

Babes on Broadway

A Metro-Goldwyn-Mayer Picture (1941)

Produced by Arthur Freed
Directed by Busby Berkeley
Screenplay by Fred Finklehoffe and Elaine Ryan
Original story by Fred Finklehoffe
Songs by E. Y. Harburg, Burton Lane, Ralph Freed, Roger Edens
* and Harold Rome*
Music Director: Georgie Stoll
Cameraman: Lester White
Editor: Frederick Y. Smith

CAST
Mickey Rooney, Judy Garland, Fay Bainter, Virginia Weidler,
Ray McDonald, Richard Quine, Donald Meek, Alexander Woollcott,
Louis Alberni, James Gleason, Emma Dunn, Frederick Burton,
Cliff Clark, William Pool, Jr.

COMMENTS
This was another M-G-M musical extravaganza, teaming Garland
and Rooney in yet another vaudeville-background story.

Judy displayed her talents as a mimic in sequences in which she impersonated the legendary actresses Blanche Ring, Sarah Bernhardt, and Fay Templeton.

What the critics said about
BABES ON BROADWAY

The New York Times

When Metro spreads itself on a production number, it invariably does a handsome job. And, it has done right nicely by the finale of *Babes on Broadway*, providing a mammoth eye-filling setting for the minstrel show which is the only racey and really entertaining episode in this otherwise dull and overly-long potpourri of comedy, drama, third-rate jokes and music. The humor department reached its zenith with the remarks, "I'm going out to get some air, I feel rather flat," which Mickey Rooney tosses off rather sheepishly. As the title of the Music Hall's new offering implies, it is basically a story about the youngsters who hang out in the Times Square theatrical precincts, hoping for that one break which will open the gates to the pearly highway of the show world.

You can observe, any day in the week, dozens of youngsters like those portrayed by Mickey Rooney and Judy Garland, congregating on the corners of Forty-fourth and Forty-fifth Streets and swapping tales of their experiences in trying to see this producer or that one. It's a sight familiar to most New Yorkers, and out of it some enterprising showman may yet evolve an entertaining musical edition of *Stage Door*. But Metro, with Mr. Rooney on its hands, just couldn't follow a simple straightforward story line. So except for an occasional and pleasant musical interruption by Miss Garland, the plot is thickened with some trite nonsense about Mickey and Judy staging a settlement house show to raise funds to send some underprivileged children to the country.

With Mickey Rooney

*With Ray McDonald, Richard Quine,
Virginia Weidler, and Fay Bainter*

And, this being a season wherein practically every Hollywood producer feels compelled to cheer on the British, a production number urging Tommy Atkins to keep his chin up is dragged into the proceedings against a montage of London Bridge, Parliament and the King's Guards. Moreover, a group of angel-faced little English visitors in America for the duration are hauled out for a microphonic cast with the folks at home. The sight of these tragic-looking youngsters, some with tears trickling down their cheeks, will touch any heart, but still this is a sequence which *Babes on Broadway* could best do without. It appeared to this observer as though Metro slipped these scenes in just to soften up the audience, an unforgivable exploitation of a tragic situation.

As usual, Mickey Rooney does not confine himself to a single characterization, but gives also his impersonations of Sir Harry Lauder (very bad), George M. Cohan (fair), a hill billy idiot (exaggerated but amusing) and a black-faced end man (lively and in the best Elks Club tradition). Though Mickey doesn't leave much room for anybody else, Judy Garland manages to stand out in the musical interludes, as does the graceful and nimble-footed Ray McDonald in a brief tap dance. (T.M.P.)

With Mickey Rooney

The New York Herald Tribune
Judging from the lines outside the Music Hall yesterday, *Babes on Broadway* was the perfect choice for a New's Year's celebration at the Radio City playhouse. It is a brash and engaging entertainment for any holiday season. Mickey Rooney and Judy Garland are getting a bit on in years to be designated as babes, but they have lost none of their shrewd showmanship in their passage through adolescence. (HOWARD BARNES)

Time
...*Babes* consumes so much celluloid at such a loud pace that it is one of the most exhausting pictures of this or any other year....

...[From a specific point] Miss Garland, now nineteen and wise to her co-star's propensity for stealing scenes, neatly takes the picture away from him. Rooney cannot sing but Judy Garland can and proves it pleasantly with such sure-fire numbers as "Waiting for the *Robert E. Lee,*" "Franklin D. Roosevelt Jones," and a new tune called "Hoe Down."

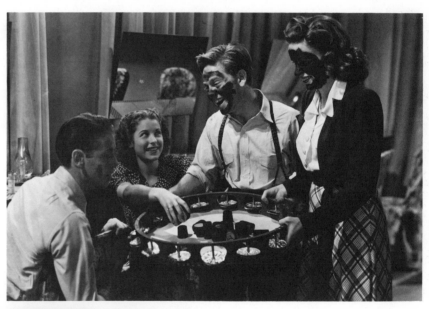

With Richard Quine and Mickey Rooney

With Mickey Rooney, Ray McDonald, and Richard Quine

We Must Have Music

This was a short subject released in 1942, utilizing a musical sequence featuring Judy Garland which had been cut out of *Ziegfeld Girl*. The short explained the importance and work of a movie studio's music department.

With Gene Kelly, rehearsing a dance routine

For Me and My Gal

A Metro-Goldwyn-Mayer Picture (1942)

Produced by Arthur Freed
Directed by Busby Berkeley
Screenplay by Richard Sherman, Fred Finklehoffe, and Sid Silvers
Original story by Howard Emmett Rogers
Song "For Me and My Gal" by George W. Meyer, Edgar Leslie,
    and E. Ray Goetz
Dance Director: Bobby Connolly
Cameraman: William Daniels
Editor: Ben Lewis
Art Director: Cedric Gibbons

CAST
Judy Garland, George Murphy, Gene Kelly, Marta Eggerth,
Ben Blue, Horace McNally, Richard Quine, Lucille Norman,
Keenan Wynn.

COMMENTS
M-G-M utilized a World War I and vaudeville theme to make
this patriotic movie during the early days of World War II.
For Me and My Gal introduced Gene Kelly to the screen.
He played a heel with whom Judy fell in love, although good
guy George Murphy kept waiting for her in the wings.

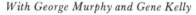

With Gene Kelly

With George Murphy and Gene Kelly

The film was criticized for having a corny plot, but no one denied the talents of the three leading performers and the entertaining qualities of the musical numbers.

This was the first film in which Judy was the only star billed above the title. M-G-M was now giving her parts which utilized her sensitive acting ability in addition to her perkiness, charm, and obvious musical talents.

The talents of Garland and Kelly complemented each other in the dramatic scenes of the film as well as in the memorable musical numbers, which included "For Me and My Gal" and "When You Wore a Tulip." Judy also sang "After You've Gone," which, along with "For Me and My Gal," she still includes in her concert repertoire.

GENE KELLY *comments:* Of all the actors in Hollywood who had seen me or known me from my Broadway days, Judy was my first booster. I was a very lucky fellow to be selected by Arthur Freed to do my first picture opposite her, and don't think that she didn't have a lot to do with that. The greatest thing I remember about Judy during the shooting of *For Me and My Gal* was her kindness. I was a good stage performer but the movies threw me. (Performing-wise, that still holds true—I'm much better on the stage than on the screen, but that's the case with a lot of people.) Judy never mentioned this to me, but very quietly helped me. I'll never forget how much I learned about movies during that first picture.

*With George Murphy, Gene Kelly,
Ben Blue, and Keenan Wynn*

GEORGE MURPHY *comments: For Me and My Gal* of course
was another excellent picture. When Judy and Gene Kelly and I
made up the triangle, I was a little downhearted about that one,
because at the outset that script had been written for me to
play the lead. But as it turned out, the powers that be at M-G-M
decided that this would be a good vehicle for Gene Kelly's
initial picture, and I was given the third part. But once again it
was exciting great fun, the picture turned out well and I have
always enjoyed tremendously the privilege of working with people
of high talent.

What the critics said about
   FOR ME AND MY GAL

The New York Times
Miss Garland is a saucy little singer and dances passably. She
handles such age flavored ballads as "After You've Gone,"

With George Murphy and Gene Kelly

With George Murphy

"Till We Meet Again," and "Smiles" with music hall lustiness and sings and dances nicely with Mr. Kelly in the title song.

The songs are good, the story maudlin—that is the long and short of it. But maybe that was vaudeville. (BOSLEY CROWTHER)

The New York Herald Tribune

Miss Garland is someone to reckon with. Of all the youngsters who have graduated into mature roles in recent years, she has the surest command of her form of make-believe.

Barring the corny aspects of the continuity [of the film], she turns in a warm, persuasive and moving portrayal of the diffident hoofer and singer who loves a heel. (HOWARD BARNES)

The New York Daily News

3½ stars . . . Judy looks thin and frail throughout the picture, but she seems to have developed enormously as an actress and entertainer since her last screen assignment. She projects the old melodies charmingly . . . and she also dances with grace. . . .

(KATE CAMERON)

Time

. . . In this nostalgic re-evocation of vaudeville's golden age and the sweeter, simpler times of World War I, Miss Garland and Mr. Kelly do a notable job.

. . . Bony-faced Judy Garland is already well graduated from a sort of female Mickey Rooney into one of the more reliable song pluggers in the business. She also begins to show symptoms of dramatic sensitiveness, discipline, and talent.

. . . The contagious little tune, "Ballin' the Jack," as delivered by Miss Garland and Mr. Kelly (helped by Miss Garland's race horse legs and by a superbly realistic vaudeville audience) is worth the price of admission.

Singing with Bob Crosby and his Bobcats

Presenting Lily Mars

A Metro-Goldwyn-Mayer Picture (1943)

Produced by Joe Pasternak
Directed by Norman Taurog
Screenplay by Richard Connell and Gladys Lehman
Based on a novel by Booth Tarkington
Songs by Walter Jurmann, Paul Francis Webster, E. Y. Harburg,
  Burton Lane, Roger Edens
Music Director: Georgie Stoll
Dance Director: Ernst Matray
Cameraman: Joseph Ruttenberg
Editor: Albert Akst
Art Director: Cedric Gibbons

With Spring Byington and the Mars family

With Fay Bainter

CAST

Judy Garland, Van Heflin, Fay Bainter, Richard Carlson, Spring Byington, Marta Eggerth, Connie Gilchrist, Leonard Kinskey, Patricia Barker, Janet Chapman, Annabelle Logan, Douglas Croft, Ray McDonald, Tommy Dorsey and his Orchestra, Bob Crosby and his Orchestra.

Doing the sleepwalking scene from Macbeth *to impress producer Van Heflin*

With Van Heflin and Richard Carlson

COMMENTS

This Booth Tarkington novel had originally been bought as a straight dramatic vehicle for Metro's rising glamour girl, Lana Turner.

It was decided to lighten the story of a small-town stagestruck girl and the new script was then considered more suitable for Judy's talents.

Joe Pasternak produced the film on a small budget, but Louis B. Mayer had him tack on a lavish production number finale showing Lily as a successful star.

JOE PASTERNAK *comments:* When I was at the recording stage and heard Judy sing, I forgot I was producing the picture and became one of the listeners. The musicians always looked forward to making a recording with her because they knew she would make a great foreground to their background. Musicians are the biggest critics in the world. If they don't think a singer is doing justice to an orchestration they feel sad. But not with her. When she did a song for me, she would go over it once or twice with Roger Edens at the piano and then, take one—finished. Perfect. She was the same way with her lines in acting— very quick.

Dancing to Tommy Dorsey and his Orchestra

Everyone felt Judy was singing to them individually. She was so convincing on screen that everybody thought she was acting for them. She was not too glamorous for the girls to dislike her or be jealous of her and she was beautiful enough for the men to fall in love with her. Those eyes—when she looked at you! She sold herself to everybody individually and collectively. You believed everything she did.

Usually when you have a great voice you're not a good actress—or when you're a good actress you don't have a great voice. She has everything in the world.

What the critics said about
PRESENTING LILY MARS

The New York Times
M-G-M . . . is again having her [Judy Garland] show off her best points in *Presenting Lily Mars*. Miss Garland is fresh and pretty—she has a perky friendliness that is completely disarming. She is a gifted young lady. [But] for all its sweetness *Presenting Lily Mars* is uninviting fare. . . . Perhaps M-G-M should let Miss Garland grow up and stay that way.

The New York Herald Tribune
Pure escapist film. . . .

Time
Presenting Lily Mars is a conventional screen version of 73-year-old Booth Tarkington's tale of a stage-struck small-town girl. This juvenile darling (Judy Garland) gets to Broadway before you can say Jake Shubert, marries a great producer (Van Heflin) and is soon seen swaying in black tulle in a super-sumptuous musical show staged by the lucky fellow.

Girl Crazy

A Metro-Goldwyn-Mayer Picture (1943)

Produced by Arthur Freed
Directed by Norman Taurog
Screenplay by Fred Finklehoffe
Based on a musical by Guy Bolton and Jack McGowan
Music and Lyrics by George and Ira Gershwin
"I Got Rhythm" number directed by Busby Berkeley
Musical adaptation: Roger Edens
Music Director: Georgie Stoll
Dance Director: Charles Walters
Cameramen: William Daniels and Robert Planck
Editor: Albert Akst
Art Director: Cedric Gibbons

CAST

Mickey Rooney, Judy Garland, Gil Stratton, Robert E. Strickland,
Rags Ragland, June Allyson, Nancy Walker, Guy Kibbee,
Frances Rafferty, Henry O'Neill, Howard Freeman, Tommy Dorsey
and his Orchestra.

COMMENTS

Movie exhibitors across the country clamored for more Garland-Rooney films, and M-G-M obliged with this movie version of the successful Gershwin stage show.

Judy sang "Embraceable You," "But Not for Me," "Bidin' My Time" and "I Got Rhythm," among others.

With Mickey Rooney and Tommy Dorsey

The elaborate finale production number was directed by Busby Berkeley.

Mickey played the part of a callow college playboy whose wealthy father sends him to a rugged boys' school in the West. He learns there are no taxis and that 6:00 A.M. is time to get up, not go to bed. He also discovers that the president of the college has a cute daughter (Judy), and that the school is in deep financial trouble. Needless to say, Mickey and Judy save the school from financial failure by staging a spectacular western jamboree.

Newcomer June Allyson appeared briefly in a musical sequence at the beginning of the film.

With Rags Ragland

Singing "Embraceable You"

ARTHUR FREED *comments:* Norman Taurog completed directing this film. I had to take Busby Berkeley off the picture because he and Judy had some kind of personality clash.

What the critics said about
GIRL CRAZY

The New York Times
Hold your hats, folks! Mickey Rooney and Judy Garland are back in town. And if at this late date there are still a few die-hards who deny that they are the most incorrigibly talented pair of youngsters in movies, then *Girl Crazy* should serve as final rebuttal.

The immortal Mickey . . . is an entertainer to his fingertips. And with Judy, who sings and acts like an earthbound angel, to temper his brashness—well, they can do almost anything they wish, and we'll like it even in spite of ourselves.

. . . Miss Garland's songs, such as "Bidin' My Time," should sooth even the most savage breast; of all the child prodigies of Hollywood, Miss Garland has outgrown her adolescence most gracefully and still sings a song with an appealing sincerity which is downright irresistible. (T.S.)

The New York Herald Tribune
. . . These two expert performers (Mickey Rooney and Judy Garland) are almost the whole show—hardly any of the footage is reeled off without one or the other of them in the spotlight.

. . . His biggest moment in the picture is a scene of clever imitations, including a tennis match announcer and a prize fight announcer.

. . . Miss Garland looks very sweet as an out-of-doors girl and she holds up her half of the show, doing for the music what Rooney does for the story. She has the help of Rooney's clowning in "Could You Use Me," an unusually cute musical number sung

With Mickey Rooney and Tommy Dorsey

With Mickey Rooney

in a jalopy along a dusty road, and in the final production number, "I've Got Rhythm."

With her excellent voice and Norman Taurog's expert staging, *Girl Crazy* is a show without a dull musical number.

. . . Chalk up another musical comedy triumph for the Rooney-Garland team. (OTIS L. GUERNSEY, JR.)

The New York Daily News

3 stars. With Mickey making the comedy both plain and fancy, Judy looking beautiful and singing plaintively, and with Tommy Dorsey playing tunes by both Gershwins . . . and with Busby Berkeley's dance routines, *Girl Crazy* is custom-made for young folks. And though not one of Mickey's and Judy's or M-G-M's best musicals, it will do quite nicely until a better one comes along. (WANDA HALE)

Time

. . . He [Rooney] is a natural dancer and comedian, and his little parlor tricks—especially one burlesque broadcast—are a pleasure to watch. Even better is Judy Garland. As sung by Cinemactress Garland, "Embraceable You" and "Bidin' My Time" become hits all over again, and the new "But Not for Me" sounds like another. Her presence is open, cheerful, and warming. If she were not so profitably good at her own game, she could obviously be a dramatic cinema actress with profit to all.

Thousands Cheer

A Metro-Goldwyn-Mayer Picture (1943)

Produced by Joe Pasternak
Directed by George Sidney
Original story and screenplay by Paul Jarrico and Richard Collins
Songs by Ferde Grofe and Harold Adamson, Lew Brown,
Ralph Freed and Burton Lane, Walter Jurmann and
Paul Francis Webster, Earl Brent and E. Y. Harburg,
Dmitri Shostakovich and Harold Rome.
Music Director: Herbert Stothart
Cameraman: George Folsey
Editor: George Boemler
Art Director: Cedric Gibbons

CAST
Kathryn Grayson, Gene Kelly, Mary Astor, John Boles, Ben Blue,
Frances Rafferty, Mary Elliott, Frank Jenks, Frank Scully,
Dick Simmons, Ben Lessey. "Guest" appearances by Judy Garland,
Mickey Rooney, Red Skelton, Eleanor Powell, Lucille Ball,
Ann Sothern, Virginia O'Brien, Lena Horne, Donna Reed,
Margaret O'Brien, and others.

John Boles, Mary Astor, Gene Kelly,
and Kathryn Grayson.

COMMENTS

Judy was a guest star in this star-studded wartime musical that
utilized most of M-G-M's imposing star roster.

She sang a specialty number by Roger Edens called "The Joint Is
Really Jumping Down at Carnegie Hall," accompanied by
Jose Iturbi, making his film debut.

The thin plot concerned a romance between Private Gene Kelly
and a Colonel's daughter, Kathryn Grayson. Mary Astor and
John Boles played her parents. The climax of the film was a big
camp show put on by movie stars. Mickey Rooney was the show's
master of ceremonies and one of the highlights of the film was
Mickey's impersonations of Clark Gable and Lionel Barrymore in a
scene from the 1938 M-G-M film, *Test Pilot*.

What the critics said about
        THOUSANDS CHEER

The New York Times
. . . It's been a long time since Metro spread itself so lavishly as in
Thousands Cheer. And it's been longer than that since the screen
provided such a veritable grab-bag of delights. Musically there is
something for all tastes, from Jose Iturbi to boogie-woogie, from
Kathryn Grayson and "Sempra Libera" to Judy Garland·and
"The Joint Is Really Jumping!"
   . . . It would have been easy for Metro's labor to result in a top-
heavy production under a less resourceful producer than
Joe Pasternak. His steadying hand is quite evident . . ." (T.M.P.)

*Gene Kelly, John Boles, and
Kathryn Grayson*

The New York Herald Tribune

... It is a prodigal and sumptuous motion picture.

Gene Kelly ... is so superb in the role of a distinguished draftee who discovers a few things about discipline and teamwork that he dominates the proceedings.

... It is Kelly who saves the picture from being merely a parade of personalities.... The specialty acts are introduced in an Army camp show ... Judy Garland is attractive as she gets Iturbi to bang out some swing rhythms on the piano.

... Perhaps you've caught on to the fact that *Thousands Cheer* has a bit of everything in it. Joe Pasternak has seen to it that most of it is good and George Sidney has staged it expansively....

(HOWARD BARNES)

Ben Blue and Gene Kelly

With Tom Drake and Margaret O'Brien

Meet Me in St. Louis

A Metro-Goldwyn-Mayer Picture (1944)

Produced by Arthur Freed
Directed by Vincente Minnelli
Screenplay by Irving Becher, Fred F. Finklehoffc
Story by Sally Benson
Score: Ralph Blane and Hugh Martin
Music Director: Georgie Stoll
Dance Director: Charles Walters
Cameraman: George Folsey
Editor: Albert Akst
Art Direction: Cedric Gibbons and Lemuel Ayers

Judy and friends

With Tom Drake

On the famous trolley

CAST

Judy Garland, Margaret O'Brien, Mary Astor, Lucille Bremer, Tom Drake, Marjorie Main, Leon Ames, Harry Davenport, June Lockhart, Henry H. Daniels, Jr., Joan Carroll, Hugh Marlowe, Robert Sully, Chill Wills.

COMMENTS

This movie, directed by Vincente Minnelli, was another milestone in Judy's career. It has been said that the role of Esther Smith, the girl with a crush on the boy next door, is Judy's favorite.

Listed as one of Variety's All-Time Box-Office Champions, this film brought Judy to the very peak of her movie career, and provided her with several of her trademark songs, including "The Trolley Song," "The Boy Next Door" and "Have Yourself a Merry Little Christmas."

The story concerns the trials and tribulations of the Smith family in turn-of-the-century St. Louis. A crisis arises when Mr. Smith (Leon Ames) announces he has been transferred to New York. He expects the family to be excited but they are depressed, since each member has his own reasons for wanting to stay in St. Louis. Also, there is the upcoming World Exposition— the St. Louis Fair.

Mrs. Smith (Mary Astor) takes the news of the move philosophically, but three of the Smith children—Rose (Lucille Bremer), Esther (Judy Garland) and little Tootie (Margaret O'Brien) are upset about the move.

The minor plot crises included: Esther being angry with the boy next door because Tootie had fibbed and told her that he unjustifiably spanked her; Rose being proposed to via long-distance telephone in the presence of the entire family; Tootie being troubled by the impending move and becoming hysterical at Christmas time, realizing it is their last Christmas in St. Louis

With Joan Carroll, Harry Davenport, Mary Astor, Lucille Bremer, and Leon Ames

With Mary Astor and Lucille Bremer

(she is soothed by Judy's poignant rendition of "Have Yourself a Merry Little Christmas").

A Mark Twain-like Halloween sequence, involving Tootie and her playmates, was another highlight of the film.

All is brought to a happy conclusion when father realizes that the best move for the Smith family would be to remain in St. Louis, and they joyfully attend the opening of the Fair.

This sentimental and charming movie, with just a wisp of plot, was based on Sally Benson's reminiscences of her childhood, which appeared as a series of stories in *The New Yorker* magazine.

A happy film of family togetherness, *Meet Me in St. Louis* found a ready audience in wartime America. It has become a classic of its genre.

ARTHUR FREED *comments: Meet Me in St. Louis* is my personal favorite. I got along wonderfully with Judy, but the only time we were ever on the outs was when we did this film. She didn't want to do the picture. Even her mother came to me about it. We bumped into some trouble with some opinions— Eddie Mannix, the studio manager, thought the Halloween sequence was wrong, but it was left in. There was a song that Rodgers and Hammerstein had written, called "Boys and Girls Like You and I," that Judy did wonderfully, but it slowed up the picture and it was cut out. After the preview of the completed film, Judy came over to me and said, "Arthur remind me not to tell you what kind of pictures to make." *Meet Me in St. Louis* was the biggest grosser Metro had up to that time, except for *Gone With the Wind*.

With Margaret O'Brien

What the critics said about
MEET ME IN ST. LOUIS

The New York Times
A charming movie. Miss Garland is full of gay exuberance as the
second sister of the lot, and sings . . . with a rich voice that grows
riper and more expressive in each new film. Her chortling of
"The Trolley Song" puts fresh zip into that inescapable tune. . . .
A ginger peachy show. (BOSLEY CROWTHER)

The New York Herald Tribune
A period family portrait . . . enchanting in its characterizations,
incident and color.

Fortunately, M-G-M has never been at a loss to have the right
performer for the right role. . . . Judy Garland is on hand to
sing several songs expertly and to give dramatic effects to the small
crises of family life. . . . Little Margaret O'Brien is wonderful.

(HOWARD BARNES)

The New York Daily News
4 Stars. . . . If you're looking for a picture that represents sheer,
unadulterated enjoyment. . . .

The story of the Smiths is told to the accompaniment of a number
of hearty laughs, one quick tear and a couple of good tunes. . . .

Judy Garland and Tom Drake . . . carry on romantically
together, and Judy of course gives out in song whenever the spirit
moves her, which is often enough to please her loyal following
but not too often to interfere seriously with the thread of the story. . . .

(KATE CAMERON)

With Tom Drake

Time

... A musical even the deaf should enjoy. They will miss some attractive tunes ... but they can watch one of the year's prettiest pictures.

... [Margaret O'Brien's] song and her cakewalk done in a nightgown at a grown-up party, are entrancing acts. Her self-terrified Halloween adventures richly set against firelight, dark streets, and the rusty confabulations of fallen leaves, bring this section of the film very near the first-rate. ...

With Robert Walker

The Clock

A Metro-Goldwyn-Mayer Picture (1945)

Produced by Arthur Freed
Directed by Vincente Minnelli
Screenplay by Robert Nathan and Joseph Schrank from a
*   story by Paul and Pauline Gallico*
Score by George Bassman
Special effects: A. Arnold Gillespie
Cameraman: George Folsey
Editor: George White
Art Directors: Cedric Gibbons and William Ferrari

CAST
Judy Garland, Robert Walker, James Gleason, Keenan Wynn,
Marshall Thompson, Lucille Gleason, Ruth Brady.

COMMENTS
This story of a couple meeting, falling in love and marrying in a
two-day period during World War II could have been a trite,
sudsy tale. Tight direction by Vincente Minnelli and beautiful

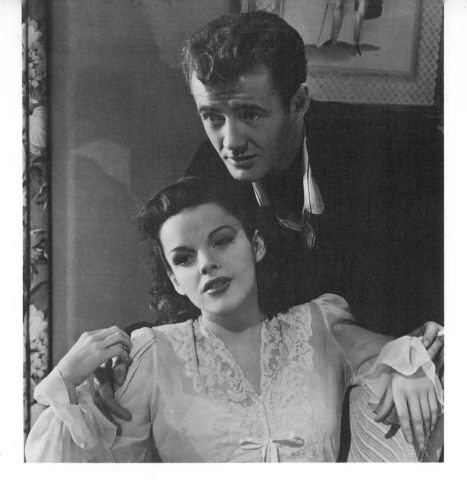

With Robert Walker

performances by Garland and Robert Walker made *The Clock* work.

The story was a timely one. The situations this young couple faced were being faced by millions of others. This was Judy's first straight dramatic role, and she didn't sing at all. Although now the story is dated, the contemporary qualities of the stars enable the film to remain a little gem.

ARTHUR FREED *comments:* Judy didn't do any more straight dramatic parts after *The Clock* because the public wanted to hear her sing, and there are so few people who can do that, while a lot of people can play dramatic parts.

I produced *The Clock* to give Judy a kick. She wanted to do a

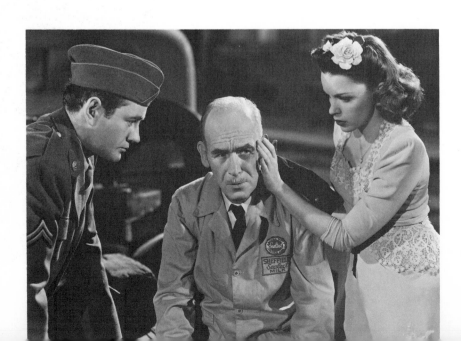

With Robert Walker and James Gleason

With Marshall Thompson and
Ruth Brady

straight picture. I started that picture with Fred Zinnemann and
had to take him off the picture because Judy and he couldn't
get along. They just didn't have any feeling for each other. I put
Vincente Minnelli on the picture. This was actually when their
big romance happened. It had begun with *Meet Me in St. Louis*
but the real thing happened during the filming of *The Clock*.

What the critics said about
THE CLOCK

The New York Times
A tender and refreshingly simple romantic drama . . . the atmosphere
of the big town has seldom been conveyed more realistically upon
the screen. . . . Robert Walker and Judy Garland (who by the
way doesn't sing a note) are the principals.
  The Clock is the kind of picture that leaves one with a warm
feeling toward his fellow man, especially towards the young folks
who today are trying to crowd a lifetime of happiness into a few
fleeting hours. (I.M.P.)

The New York Herald Tribune
A sincere and touching examination of the war-time marriage
problem. Miss Garland, who doesn't sing a note in *The Clock*, works
considerable sympathy into her role. She . . . maintains the
impression of variety in the continual boy-girl relationship. . . .
She reacts to the ugliness and red tape of a municipal wedding and
then keeps the relationship from becoming too sugary when the
disappointment is amended. (OTIS L. GUERNSEY)

With Robert Walker and unidentified
players

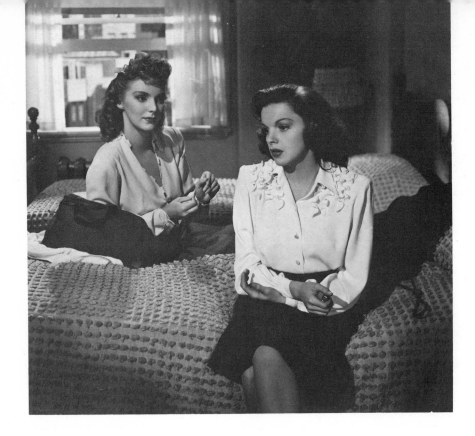

With Ruth Brady

The New York Daily News
3½ stars . . . *The Clock* . . . is the sweetest, most tender comedy-drama yet produced about a soldier and a girl.

Judy Garland and Robert Walker are perfectly cast as the modest, sincere girl and the shy, sincere boy.

To Vincente Minnelli goes the credit for the film's many appealing qualities. He has directed the love scenes with great tenderness. And the humor he has worked into the plot is so carefully and cleverly done that many scenes without words stand out like animated paintings and cartoons. . . . (WANDA HALE)

Time
The Clock, at its best, is so good that it inspires ingratitude for not being great. Its basic story is about as simple and moving as they come.

. . . Director Minnelli's talents are so many sided and generous that he turns even the most over-contrived romanticism into something memorable. He has brought the budding dramatic talents of . . . Judy Garland into unmistakable bloom. He has helped give Robert Walker an honest, touching dignity in place of the shucks-fellers cuteness he has sometimes seemed doomed to. He has used most of his bit players and extras and crowds and streets so well that time and again you wonder whether some swarming multitudinously human scenes were made in the actual city, with only a few of the actors aware of concealed cameras. . . .

[Minnelli's] semi-surrealist juxtapositions, accidental or no, help turn *The Clock* into a rich image of a great city. His love of mobility, of snooping and sailing and drifting and drooping his camera booms and dollies, makes *The Clock,* largely boom shot, one of the most satisfactorily flexible movies since Friedrich Murnau's epoch-making *The Last Laugh.* . . .

Angela Lansbury and the Dancehall Girls

The Harvey Girls

A Metro-Goldwyn-Mayer Picture (1946)

Produced by Arthur Freed
Associate Producer: Roger Edens
Directed by George Sidney
Screenplay by Edmund Beloin and Nathaniel Curtis from a
*   story by Samuel Hopkins Adams, Eleanore Griffin, and*
*   William Rankin*
Songs by Johnny Mercer, Harry Warren
Musical Director: Lennie Hayton
Special Effects: Warren Newcombe
Cameraman: George Folsey
Editor: Albert Akst
Art Direction: Cedric Gibbons and William Ferrari

CAST
Judy Garland, John Hodiak, Ray Bolger, Angela Lansbury,
Preston Foster, Virginia O'Brien, Kenny Baker, Marjorie Main,
Chill Wills, Selena Royle, Cyd Charisse, Ruth Brady, Jack Lambert,
Edward Earle, Morris Ankrum, William "Bill" Phillips, Ben Carter,
Norman Leavitt, Horace (Stephen) McNally.

COMMENTS
World War II was over, movies were bigger than ever and M-G-M
pulled out all the stops, showcasing Judy in this lavish Technicolor
musical comedy set against the background of the old West.

With John Hodiak

It was a fictional account of Fred Harvey's traveling waitresses, in which Judy warbled the hit song "On the Atchison, Topeka and the Santa Fe." She also tamed the West and won the sophisticated cowboy, John Hodiak.

Young Angela Lansbury and an unknown dancer named Cyd Charisse were featured in the cast.

The Harvey Girls is listed by *Variety* as one of the All-Time Box-office Champions.

With Virginia O'Brien and Cyd Charisse

Angela Lansbury and the Dancehall Girls

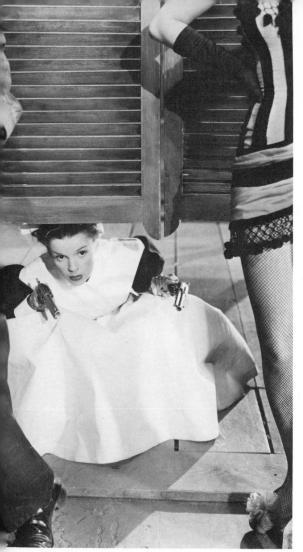

What the critics said about
THE HARVEY GIRLS

The New York Times
An abundance of chromatic spectacle and an uncommonly good score.

Miss Garland of course is at the center of most of the activity and handles herself in pleasing fashion—up to and including the high notes.

A rather lofty tribute to Fred Harvey's girls, but it's a show.
(BOSLEY CROWTHER)

The New York Herald Tribune
A great big animated picture postcard. Judy Garland is the film's bright...star. Miss Garland is effectively glamorized in get-ups of the '90's and sings her songs pleasantly. Hodiak gives her valuable dramatic support. *The Harvey Girls* is a perfect demonstration of what Hollywood can do with its vast resources when it wants to be really showy.... Pretty girls...period sets and costumes... lilting tunes...super-speedy dance shuffles. (HOWARD BARNES)

The New York Daily News
3 Stars.... a nostalgic whiff of the old west. Judy...sings several sentimental ballads, as well as the "On the Atchison, Topeka and the Santa Fe" number. Her chief support in the way of real entertainment comes from Ray Bolger. (KATE CAMERON)

Time
The Harvey Girls is a Technicolored musical celebrating the coming of chastity, clean silverware, and crumbless tablecloths to the pioneer Southwest. The bearers of this culture, according to evidence presented here, were waitresses....

The Harvey Girls is good fun in spots. Miss Garland doesn't seem as recklessly happy as she was in St. Louis but she still appears to be having a pretty fine time.

*With Stephen McNally
and Angela Lansbury*

Ziegfeld Follies of 1946

A Metro-Goldwyn-Mayer Picture (1946)

Produced by Arthur Freed
Directed by Vincente Minnelli
Musical Adaptation: Roger Edens
Musical Director: Lennie Hayton
Dance Director: Robert Alton
Cameramen: George Folsey and Charles Rosher
Editor: Albert Akst
Art Direction: Cedric Gibbons, Merrill Pye and Jack Martin Smith

CAST
Fred Astaire, Lucille Ball, Lucille Bremer, Fanny Brice,
Judy Garland, Kathryn Grayson, Lena Horne, Gene Kelly,
James Melton, Victor Moore, Red Skelton, Esther Williams,
William Powell, Edward Arnold, Marion Bell, Bunin's Puppets,
Cyd Charisse, Hume Cronyn, William Frawley, Robert Lewis,
Virginia O'Brien, Keenan Wynn.

Lucille Ball in production number

Fred Astaire and Lucille Bremer

COMMENTS
Another of M-G-M's all-star musical revues, filmed in 1944, '45, and '46.

Judy appeared in the musical sequence entitled "The Interview," a clever satire on a publicity interview given by a Hollywood movie star. A film piece in *The New York Times* by Bosley Crowther described Judy as "giving promise of a talent approaching that of Beatrice Lillie or Gertrude Lawrence."

The film is cited by *Variety* as one of the All-Time Box-office Champions.

ARTHUR FREED *comments:* Judy loved doing sophisticated parts like "The Interview" sequence in this film. But mind you, that particular number was not one of her biggest successes except with a certain group.

The New York Times
The film's best numbers . . . are a couple of comedy skits, especially one done by Red Skelton. Fanny Brice plays a Bronx hausfrau quite . . . funnily. Judy Garland is also amusing as a movie queen giving an interview. *Ziegfeld Follies* is entertaining—and that's what it's meant to be! (BOSLEY CROWTHER)

The New York Herald Tribune
The fashion of the big screen revue has seen its day. The person

Judy in "The Interview" sequence

Judy in "The Interview" sequence

who gets the worst flogging in the deal is Judy Garland. Wound up in a sketch called The Interview, Miss Garland has some mighty unpleasant stuff to do (JOE PIHODNA)

Newsweek

. . . At least three of the numbers would highlight any review on stage or screen. In "A Great Lady Has an Interview," Judy Garland, with six leading men, displays an unexpected flair for occupational satire.

With "Numbers Please" Keenan Wynn demonstrates, once again, that he is one of Hollywood's foremost comedians . . . But the dance act for the archives is "The Babbitt and the Bromide." . . . Fred Astaire and Gene Kelly trade taps and double-takes to a photo finish. . . .

Publicity picture showing all the stars of Till the Clouds Roll By. *Standing: Robert Walker. First row: June Allyson, Lucille Bremer, Judy, Kathryn Grayson. Second row: Van Heflin, Lena Horne, Van Johnson, Tony Martin, Dinah Shore. Bottom: Frank Sinatra*

Till the Clouds Roll By

A Metro-Goldwyn-Mayer-Picture (1946)

Produced by Arthur Freed
Directed by Richard Whorf
Screenplay by Myles Connolly and Jean Halloway
Story by Guy Bolton
Adaptation by George Wells
Musical Direction: Lennie Hayton
Orchestrations: Conrad Salinger
Cameramen: Harry Stradling and George Folsey
Editor: A. Akst
Art Direction: Cedric Gibbons

Singing "Look for the Silver Lining"

CAST

June Allyson, Lucille·Bremer, Judy Garland, Kathryn Grayson, Van Heflin, Lena Horne, Van Johnson, Tony Martin, Dinah Shore, Frank Sinatra, Robert Walker, Gower Champion, Cyd Charisse, Harry Hayden, Paul Langton, Angela Lansbury, Paul Macey, Ray McDonald, Mary Nash, Virginia O'Brien, Dorothy Patrick, Caleb Peterson, William Phillips, Joan Wells, The Wilde Twins.

COMMENTS

Judy's scenes as Marilyn Miller in this star-studded cavalcade were directed by Vincente Minnelli, and her musical numbers, "Look for the Silver Lining" and "Who," provided the film with its few highlights.

With Robert Walker

With chorus

Robert Walker portrayed Jerome Kern, and the fabled Kern melodies were sung by a glittering array of M-G-M's stars.

It was rather tedious, except for some of the musical numbers. It failed in its attempt to establish Lucille Bremer—a good dancer, but a poor actress—as a star.

ARTHUR FREED *comments:* On film, Judy had a great warmth. Any song she ever sang, you always felt she was singing it to you personally. For example, in this picture, "Look for the Silver Lining." I think this is one of the big reasons why she has the big following she has today.

What the critics said about
     TILL THE CLOUDS ROLL BY

The New York Times
Why did Metro . . . cook up such a phony yarn. . . . Why couldn't it simply have given us more such enjoyable things as Judy Garland playing Marilyn Miller and singing the melodious "Sunny" and "Who?" (BOSLEY CROWTHER)

...A glamorized biography of the late Jerome Kern.... Some twenty-five of the pleasanter personalities M-G-M owns or could snag for the occasion are on hand, and they go through about two dozen of Kern's graceful, contagious tunes, neck-deep in sumptuous production. Van Johnson does a highly self-appreciative song and dance—looking, unfortunately, a little as if he should be carrying a roast apple in his mouth. Judy Garland is charming as the late Marilyn Miller and still more charming when she sings "Who." Dinah Shore gives special warmth to "They Didn't Believe Me" and "The Last Time I Saw Paris." Lena Horne sings "Can't Help Loving Dat Man" and "Why Was I Born" with as much careful intensity as if she were expounding existentialism....

...The picture, in fact, is little more than a series of production numbers of Kern songs which, luckily, are good enough to stand on their own.... The cast is impressive... Van Heflin... gains what acting honors are to be had....

Singing "Who"

The Pirate

A Metro-Goldwyn-Mayer Picture (1948)

Produced by Arthur Freed
Directed by Vincente Minnelli
Screenplay by Albert Hackett and Frances Goodrich from a
  play by S. N. Behrman
Music by Cole Porter
Musical Direction: Lennie Hayton
Photography: Harry Stradling
Editor: Blanche Sewell
Art Direction: Cedric Gibbons and Jack Martin Smith

With Gene Kelly singing "Mack the Black"

With Gene Kelly

CAST

Judy Garland, Gene Kelly, Walter Slezak, Gladys Cooper, Reginald Owen, George Zucco, Nicholas Brothers, Lester Allen, Lola Deem, Ellen Ross, Mary Jo Ellis, Jean Dean, Marion Murray, Ben Lessy, Jerry Bergen, Val Zetz, Goldsmith Brothers, Cully Richards.

COMMENTS

The Pirate had a witty script, adapted from the play by S. N. Behrman (played on the Broadway stage by Alfred Lunt and Lynn Fontanne). The picture was not a box-office bonanza, despite a Cole Porter score and excellent direction by Vincente Minnelli. Judy and Gene Kelly sparkled, especially in their rendition of "Be a Clown."

ARTHUR FREED *comments:* When we did *The Pirate,* Judy wasn't feeling well. The last number we shot was "Be a Clown," and Judy rehearsed for that for four hours before we started shooting. I think it's one of the best pictures she's done. It didn't lose money, but it wasn't the success I hoped it would be. I think one of the reasons was the public didn't want to see Judy as a sophisticate. I think today *The Pirate* would be a hit. It was twenty years ahead of its time.

The New York Herald Tribune
A gala screen musical has been made out of S. N. Behrman's
romantic costume play, *The Pirate*. M-G-M has played considerable
hob with the original Alfred Lunt-Lynn Fontanne starring vehicle.
Most of it is to the good. At the Music Hall there is more
dancing than script; more production pomp than sensible staging.
But with Gene Kelly hoofing like a dervish, Judy Garland changing
character at the drop of a hat, and resplendent trappings, the show
is bouncing and beautiful. Occasionally the Behrman wit crackles
through the proceedings to advantage. The important thing is
that his original dramatic notion has inspired a fetching film.

Kelly has a particular triumph in the production. Where Lunt
had to learn some vaudeville tricks for the stage offering, Kelly
takes a variety of them in full stride, while acting with sly
authority in the straight passages of the farce. He dominates the
doings in *The Pirate* in no uncertain manner. Miss Garland
dances in a trance, sings pleasantly and does a superb job of crockery
smashing in the scene in which she discovers that her beloved
pirate is only an itinerant mummer. Although the stars are backed
up by hundreds of extras and panoply galore, they are in charge
of *The Pirate* on the screen as surely as were Lunt and Fontanne
behind footlights. (HOWARD BARNES)

With Gene Kelly

The New York Times
The difference between the talents of Gene Kelly and
Judy Garland and those of Alfred Lunt and Lynn Fontanne is as
night is to day. *The Pirate* was fashioned most purposefully for
the celebrated pair from Genesee Depot, so Metro-Goldwyn-Mayer
wisely set about making little, but significant, changes here and
there in filming this fantastic conglomeration of legerdemain,
dancing and romance. *The Pirate*, which came yesterday to the
Radio City Music Hall, is a dazzling, spectacular extravaganza,
shot through with all the colors of the rainbow and then some that
are Technicolor patented.

It takes this mammoth show some time to generate a full head
of steam, but when it gets rolling it's thoroughly delightful.
However, the momentum is far from steady and the result is a
lopsided entertainment that is wonderfully flamboyant in its high
spots and bordering on tedium elsewhere.

Miss Garland teams nicely with Mr. Kelly, singing or dancing,
and she throws herself with verve into a wild, slapstick exercise,
tossing everything that's not nailed down at the dashing trouper.
It's funny, but a mite overdone. However, the finale, which
finds the pair on the threshold of living happily ever after, is a
lively roughhouse session of clowning set to the tune of "Be a Clown,"
easily the best of Cole Porter's several songs. Walter Slezak as
Don Pedro, Gladys Cooper as Aunt Inez and George Zucco as the
viceroy do well by their roles. But *The Pirate* is Mr. Kelly's picture

Singing "Love of My Life" to Gene Kelly

"Be a Clown"

and he gives it all he has, which is considerable and worthy of attention. (T.M.P.)

Time

...As an all-out try at artful movie making, this is among the most interesting pictures of the year. Unluckily, much of the considerable artistry that has gone into this production collides head-on with artiness or is spoiled by simpler kinds of miscalculation....

The movie extension of this S. N. Behrman play into a musical spectacular involves songs and lyrics by Cole Porter, dances designed by Gene Kelly and Robert Alton, and the direction of Miss Garland's husband, the talented Vincente Minnelli.

...Miss Garland's tense, ardent straightforwardness is sometimes very striking.

...The total effect of the picture is "entertainment" troubled by delusions of "art" and vice-versa....

Newsweek

...With Judy Garland and Gene Kelly pitching energetically into the lead roles...*Pirate* is one of the most delightful musicals to hit the screen in a month of Sundays....*The Pirate* is a rare and happy combination of expert dancing, catchy tunes, and utterly unbelievable plot which manages to achieve pure escapism without becoming either sentimental or corny.

With Fred Astaire

Easter Parade

A Metro-Goldwyn-Mayer Picture (1948)

Produced by Arthur Freed
Directed by Charles Walters
Screenplay by Sidney Shelton, Frances Goodrich and Albert Hackett
*   from a story by Frances Goodrich and Albert Hackett*
Lyrics and Music by Irving Berlin
Musical Direction: Johnny Green
Director of Photography: Harry Stradling
Editor: A. Akst
Art Direction: Cedric Gibbons and Jack Martin Smith

CAST
Judy Garland, Fred Astaire, Peter Lawford, Ann Miller,
Jules Munshin, Clinton Sundburg, Jeni LeGon.

With Fred Astaire, singing and dancing "When the Midnight Choo-Choo Leaves for Alabam'"

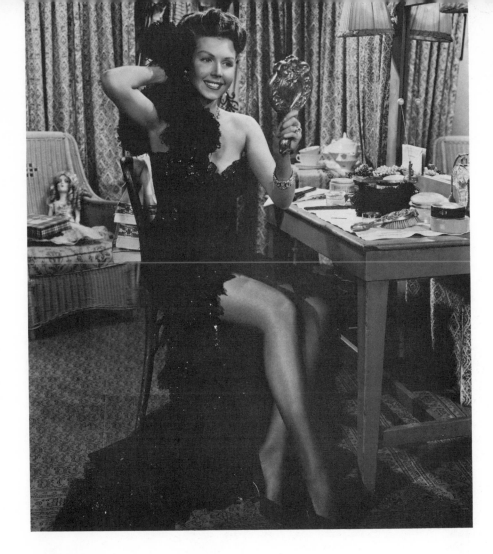

Ann Miller

COMMENTS

Judy got top billing over Fred Astaire in this highly successful Irving Berlin musical. She played a small-time singer-dancer in a chorus, picked, on a bet, by big-time dancer Astaire to be the successor of his ex-dancing partner Ann Miller. Charles Walters, former dancer and M-G-M dance director, made his directorial debut with this film. *Easter Parade* is listed by *Variety* as one of the All-Time Box-office Champions.

With Fred Astaire

With Fred Astaire, singing "Easter Parade"

With Fred Astaire, singing "We're a Couple of Swells"

ARTHUR FREED *comments:* Judy loved working with Fred Astaire. She was just as fast on the pickup in dancing as she was in singing. She rehearsed less than anybody in the world.

The only reason Irving Berlin let me buy *Easter Parade* was because he wanted to do a picture with Judy. That's how the picture started.

E. Y. HARBURG *comments:* Judy was great in *Easter Parade*. She was adorable. When anybody dances with Fred Astaire, you don't see anybody but Fred. But when Judy danced with him, you looked at her.

What the critics said about
EASTER PARADE

The New York Herald Tribune
Irving Berlin, Fred Astaire, and Judy Garland have pooled their musical and dancing talents in a smart and fetching screen carnival. . . . Astaire is hoofing more superbly than ever and Miss Garland is giving him the staunchest of support. Miss Garland

With Peter Lawford

has matured to a remarkable degree in *Easter Parade* . . . a
handsome and knowing actress. Her latest film performance is
altogether her best. (HOWARD BARNES)

The New York Times
Miss Garland is a competent trouper, nimble on her feet and
professional sounding vocally, but somehow we feel that Miss Miller
pairs better with Astaire.

The New York Daily News
3½ Stars. . . . Just what the moving picture shoppers on Broadway
have been looking for . . . gay, witty, tuneful and filled with the
magic rhythm of Fred Astaire's and Ann Miller's dancing and with
Judy Garland's warbling of Berlin's enticing tunes. . . . Judy,
wan and frail, needs a little more flesh on her bones to give her
more verve and bring her up to her old standard as an
entertainer. . . . (KATE CAMERON)

Newsweek
. . . A sprightly, beguiling musical that makes a strong bid for the
season's honors in its field. . . . The story is designed to keep
Astaire dancing and to provide for a wide variety of dance numbers,
a graceful ballroom *pas de deux* with Miss Miller, delightful
hoofing, singing, and witty sayings routines with Miss Garland,
and finally some brilliant solos. . . .

[147]

Words and Music

A Metro-Goldwyn-Mayer Picture (1948)

Produced by Arthur Freed
Directed by Norman Taurog
Screenplay by Fred Finklehoffe
Story by Guy Bolton and Jean Halloway
Musical Direction: Lennie Hayton
Photography: Charles Rosher, Harry Stradling
Editors: A. Akst and Ferris Webster
Art Direction: Cedric Gibbons and Jack Martin Smith

With Mickey Rooney

CAST

June Allyson, Perry Como, Judy Garland, Lena Horne, Gene Kelly,
Mickey Rooney, Tom Drake, Ann Sothern, Cyd Charisse,
Betty Garrett, Janet Leigh, Marshall Thompson, Mel Torme,
Vera-Ellen, Jeanette Nolan, Richard Quine, Clinton Sundburg,
Dee Turnell, Harry Antrim, Ilka Grunning, Emory Parnell,
Helen Spring, Edward Earle.

With Mickey Rooney

COMMENTS

Mickey Rooney and Tom Drake were Richard Rodgers and
Lorenz Hart in . . . yes . . . another of M-G-M's all-star musicals.
Judy played herself in a party sequence and belted out "Johnny
One Note." With Mickey Rooney she sang and danced "I Wish
I Were in Love Again." This song had been cut from the
original score of their 1939 hit, "Babes in Arms," because it was
then considered too sophisticated.

With Mickey Rooney

The New York Times

Fortunately, the wonderful music of Richard Rodgers and the late Lorenz Hart is treated with passable justice in *Words and Music,* which came to the Music Hall yesterday. Fortunately, too, the general public is not likely to be too much concerned about the actual whys and wherefores of these two popular song-writers' careers. Otherwise, this picture, which is supposed to celebrate this famous team, its music and activities, might be hooted right out of the house.

For the painful fact is that *Words and Music,* however much it may be the star-studded Technicolored feature of the Music Hall's come-all Christmas show, is a patently juvenile specimen of musical biography, as far from the facts in its reporting as it is standard in its sentimental plot. And as much as it may be crowded with Metro's jostling boys and girls, who come bouncing in at odd moments to do their acts and disappear, it is played with fantastic incompetence by Tom Drake and Mickey Rooney in the principal roles. . . . As for the others in the picture—Judy Garland for a couple of songs, Ann Sothern, Mel Torme and Marshall Thompson— the best to be said for them is that they do their jobs as directed in a disappointingly unimaginative show.

The New York Herald Tribune
It is a sumptuous production, employing a number of M-G-M
acting notables in richly festooned settings. For all its pomp and
circumstance, it is the score of nostalgic Rodgers and Hart
songs that lends some distinction to the show. The songs are as
wonderful as ever, whether they are sung by Lena Horne,
Perry Como, June Allyson and Judy Garland, or danced to by
Gene Kelly and Vera-Ellen in an effective screen reproduction of
"Slaughter on Tenth Avenue."

As for the personal story of a composer who became happy as
well as famous and a lyricist who doomed himself to death at the
height of his career, it is both silly and saccharine. . . . Over-
production has seriously marred what might have proved an
interesting musical melange. All of the performers seem self-conscious
about their Technicolor make-ups and the slant of their profiles.
Norman Taurog has missed no chance for extravagant ensembles in
his staging. *Words and Music* gives a slight hint of the wandering
minstrel who should have been the focal point of an engrossing
story accompaniment to great songs. The songs save it from ennui.

(HOWARD BARNES)

Time
. . . Outrageously cast as lyricist Hart, Mickey Rooney runs his own
narrow gamut between the brash and the maudlin, tottering
finally to a ludicrous death on the rain-pelted sidewalk. As Rodgers,
young Tom Drake looks and behaves like a well-mannered New
Haven undergraduate. Between them, they hold up a limb
plot line. . . .

With Mickey Rooney

Newsweek

...*Words and Music* is a good show when it sticks to the business implied in its title.

Lena Horne . . . brings the film to its toes with her vocalization of "Where or When" and "The Lady Is a Tramp." . . . Judy Garland . . . keeps it there with "I Wish I Were in Love Again" and "Johnny One Note."

With Mickey Rooney

In the Good Old Summertime

A Metro-Goldwyn-Mayer Picture (1949)

Produced by Joe Pasternak
Directed by Robert Z. Leonard
Screenplay by Samson Raphaelson
Story by Mikolas Laszlo
Music Director: George Stoll
Photography: Harry Stradling
Editor: Adrienne Fazan
Art Direction: Cedric Gibbons and Randall Duell

CAST

Judy Garland, Van Johnson, S. Z. "Cuddles" Sakall,
Spring Byington, Buster Keaton, Clinton Sundburg, Marcia Van
Dyke, Lillian Bronson.

COMMENTS

Judy replaced June Allyson, who was pregnant, in this musical
version of the Margaret Sullivan-James Stewart 1940 hit, *The Shop
Around the Corner*. It is the tale of a young couple who are
antagonistic fellow workers but who unknowingly carry on a
correspondence love affair. The film's locale was changed from

With Van Johnson

modern-day Hungary to turn-of-the-century Chicago. Despite the slump period movies were undergoing, this film was a box-office success.

To utilize the talents of the stars, "The Shop Around the Corner" became a music store. The proprietor of the music store was the lovable Viennese character, S. Z. "Cuddles" Sakall. Judy portrayed the young salesgirl who sang, played the piano and harp and sold sheet music of the latest pop songs.

While she and her co-worker (Van Johnson) disliked each other intensely, each carried on a correspondence love affair with their ideal mate. Of course, they were corresponding with each other. Other store employees included Spring Byington, Buster Keaton, and Clinton Sundberg. A subplot concerned Cuddles's romance with Spring Byington.

The plot was light and frothy, with the usual predictable mixups and happy ending.

With Van Johnson and S. Z. "Cuddles" Sakall

The studio succeeded in its attempt to make the film a vehicle for the stars' talents. Judy belted out "Play That Barbershop Chord" and Eva Tanguay's old hit, "I Don't Care," and she warbled "Meet Me Tonight in Dreamland." In this picture the tone of her voice was particularly warm, solid and "brilliant."

The boy-next-door appeal of Van Johnson, the warm, bumbling humor of "Cuddles" Sakall, the deadpan facility of Buster Keaton and the charm of Spring Byington all worked together to make *In the Good Old Summertime* another effective M-G-M family picture.

JOE PASTERNAK *comments:* Judy looked at a script once—

With Buster Keaton, S. Z. "Cuddles" Sakall, and Van Johnson

and never flubbed a line. She learned a musical number in no time and she gave it her all. Very seldom did you have to make two takes with her. This was very unusual—a normal musical comedy star would take three or four weeks to learn a number. What we did was to have a stand-in go through it. Judy used to watch it once or twice, then do the number.

Some stars never looked at the day's rushes. I don't think Clark Gable or Spencer Tracy ever looked at them. Sometimes Judy would look at the rushes—sometimes she liked herself and sometimes she didn't—but she was never right, because her own conception of herself was not as good as the director's, mine or the audience's. She was never completely satisfied.

What the critics said about
IN THE GOOD OLD SUMMERTIME

The New York Daily News
3 stars. . . . Looking much sturdier than she did in her last screen appearance, Judy performs the role of the ambitious heroine with some of her old time verve. She also sings the title song and several other old favorites with unusual effectiveness. (KATE CAMERON)

Newsweek
Films based on musical nostalgia have so often been saddled with silly plots that even Technicolor and important casts couldn't keep them afloat. Hence, the unflagging sparkle of *Summertime* comes as a pleasant surprise. . . . Miss Garland's voice—as appealing as ever—this time plays second fiddle to one of her best straight comedy performances.

With Gene Kelly, Phil Silvers, Hans Conreid, Marjorie Main, Gloria DeHaven, and group (Carlton Carpenter in right foreground)

Summer Stock

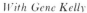

With Gene Kelly

A Metro-Goldwyn-Mayer Picture (1950)

Produced by Joe Pasternak
Directed by Charles Walters
Screenplay by George Wells and Sy Gomberg
Story by Sy Gomberg
Music Director: Johnny Green
Photography by Robert Planck
Editor: A. Akst
Art Direction: Cedric Gibbons and J. M. Smith

CAST
Judy Garland, Gene Kelly, Eddie Bracken, Gloria de Haven,
Marjorie Main, Phil Silvers, Ray Collins, Nita Bieber,
Carlton Carpenter, Hans Conreid.

COMMENTS
Judy's last M-G-M picture teamed her again with Gene Kelly, and again featured a story about show business people. It too made money at the box office, which not very many films were doing at that time.

With Gene Kelly

Summer Stock presented Judy as a New England farm owner whose sister Abigail (Gloria de Haven) had theatrical ambitions. Without telling Judy, Abigail invited Gene Kelly, Phil Silvers, Hans Conreid and their summer stock troupe to take over Judy's barn as a summer theatre and live at the farm during rehearsals.

Judy and her housekeeper (Marjorie Main) were at first antagonistic towards the actors, but by film's end Judy replaced

With Gene Kelly

her sister as star of the show and Gene Kelly replaced Eddie Bracken as Judy's beau.

Director Charles Walters staged the dances and musical numbers cleverly, and while *Summer Stock* was not a classic, it was pleasant and well received.

JOE PASTERNAK *comments:* By this time she was more difficult to work with—but though she might become lazy, it never showed on screen. She still gave the same good performance.

When the picture was over, we discovered we needed another number. She had lost about fifteen or twenty pounds between the two months before we had finished cutting the picture and the time she did the last number—"Get Happy"—and looked so beautiful that everybody thought it was a stock shot [EDITOR'S NOTE: a sequence from an earlier film]. When we previewed the picture with an audience, they didn't care what she looked like. They loved her. I don't think any actress was as loved by the American public as Judy.

When I worked with Judy, a single rose was placed in her dressing room each day that she worked. On the card attached to it, simply the words, "Good Morning, Judy Dear." For years she tried and made every effort to find out who had sent these roses but never found out until she opened an engagement in London at the Palladium. My representative in London also had the single rose placed in her dressing room there—with the same note, only that it was changed to "Good Evening, Judy Dear." She questioned my representative and that is how she finally discovered who this admirer was—and, of course, it was me.

Singing "Get Happy"

What the critics said about
SUMMER STOCK

The New York Daily News
If audience reaction is an indication, *Summer Stock,* the new
Judy Garland-Gene Kelly film, will give the year's best musical
comedies lively competition.

Judy and Gene are in fine form. Their singing and dancing, alone
and together, brought hearty applause from enthusiastic spectators
attending the first showing of the M-G-M Technicolor picture
at the Capitol Theatre. . . . Both are able players, which makes it
as much a pleasure to see them act as it is to hear them sing or
watch them dance. (WANDA HALE)

Time
Summer Stock, no great shakes as a cinemusical, serves nonetheless
as a welcome reminder of Judy Garland's unerring way with a
song. Ill, and in and out of trouble with her studio, Actress Garland
has been off the screen since last year's *In the Good Old
Summertime.* A rest cure left her chubbily overweight for her first
return performance. But none of it seems to have affected her
ability as one of Hollywood's few triple-threat girls. Thanks to
Actress Garland's singing, dancing, and acting (and some
imaginative dancing by Gene Kelly) the picture seems considerably
better than it is. . . .

Though the show's only distinguished song is an old one,
"Get Happy," her voice and showmanlike delivery do wonders
for the whole score.

A Star Is Born

A Warner Brothers Release; a Transcona Enterprises Production, (1954)

Produced by Sidney Luft
Directed by George Cukor
Screenplay by Moss Hart
Based on a screenplay by Dorothy Parker, Alan Campbell
    and Robert Carson
Story by William A. Wellman and Robert Carson
Music by Harold Arlen
Lyrics by Ira Gershwin
"Born in a Trunk" number by Leonard Gershe
Musical Direction: Ray Heindorf
Associate Producer: Vern Alves
Cinematographer: Sam Leavitt
Editor: Folmar Blangsted
Art Direction: Malcolm Bert

CAST
Judy Garland, James Mason, Jack Carson, Charles Bickford,
Tom Noonan, Lucy Marlowe, Amanda Blake, Irving Blake,
Hazel Shermet, Wilton Graff, Grady Sutton, James Brown,
Lotus Robb.

COMMENTS
Judy's triumphant return to films was in this remake of
David O. Selznick's 1937 *A Star Is Born*. It surpassed the original

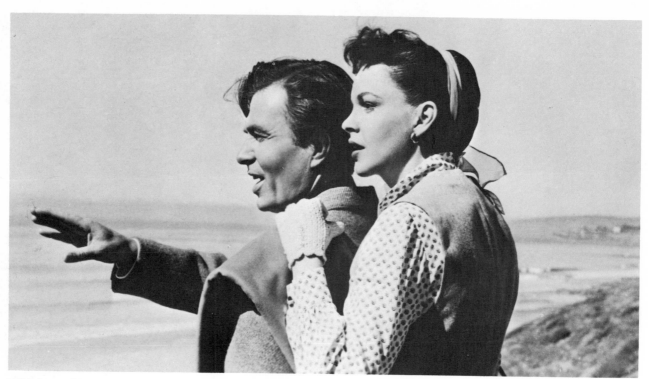

With James Mason

and offered a new dimension to the story via its now classic score by Harold Arlen and Ira Gershwin. "The Man That Got Away" and "Born in a Trunk" were added to Judy's repertoire of trademark songs.

The film enabled her to exhibit the full range of her dramatic and vocal abilities. While musicals of the '30's and '40's were escapist and frothy fare, this 1954 *A Star Is Born* was a hard-hitting and realistic portrayal of show business people. It enabled Judy to be believable in a totally believable musical drama.

The 18-minute musical sequence, "Born in a Trunk," tracing the "overnight" success story of a typical vaudevillian, had biographical overtones. It ranks as one of the finest and most distinctive musical film sequences.

Judy was nominated for an Oscar for her performance in *A Star Is Born*, but the award that year went to Grace Kelly, for *The Country Girl*.

Briefly, *A Star Is Born's* story concerns Esther Blodgett (Judy Garland), a band singer discovered by aging and slipping movie idol Norman Maine (James Mason), on the evening when Esther saves him from making a drunken spectacle of himself in front of a gala benefit audience. Later that same evening, and sober, Maine tracks her down and hears her sing, recognizing in her voice the qualities of true greatness. Eventually, he helps her to success and stardom. When the star of a major musical film walks out, Maine persuades Oliver (Charles Bickford), the warm-hearted head of the studio, to cast Esther in the part.

Esther Blodgett becomes Vicki Lester, and an overnight success in films. She marries Norman and they are very much in love.

With James Mason

Happiness is theirs for a brief period, and Norman stops his drinking.

But the studio and its press agent, Libby (Jack Carson), begin concentrating on Vicki, as Norman Maine's career has eclipsed.

Norman returns to his drinking and eventually has to be put into an institution. After Norman humiliates Vicki and himself before a national television audience on the night she wins an Academy Award, Vicki begins to think that the only way to save Norman and her marriage is to give up her career.

Norman's final degradation comes after a three-day drinking binge and a heartbreaking scene in a Los Angeles jail when he is publicly reprimanded by the judge and put in Vicki's custody.

When Vicki informs Oliver of her decision to end her career and devote her life to Norman, Norman overhears the conversation and faces the reality of the situation. He pretends to be well, requests her to sing a song for him and tells her he's going for a short swim. He walks into the sea and drowns himself.

After Maine's death, Vicki is totally despondent until a lifelong

With James Mason

friend (Tom Noonan) persuades her that Norman sacrificed his
life so that she could fulfill the great potential she had been given.

In the final poignant scene at the gala benefit at which she is
the guest of honor, she gives full credit to her husband by introducing
herself not as Vicki Lester but as Mrs. Norman Maine.

A Star Is Born was the apex of Judy Garland's film career.

What the critics said about
A STAR IS BORN

The New York Times
Those who have blissful recollections of David O. Selznick's
A Star Is Born . . . may get set for a new experience. . . . One of the
grandest heartbreak dramas that has drenched the screen in years.
A sweet and touching love story that Moss Hart has smoothly
modernized. . . . Cukor . . . gets performances from Miss Garland
and Mr. Mason that make the heart flutter and bleed.
Miss Garland is excellent in all things but most winningly perhaps
in the song "Here's What I'm Here For," wherein she dances,
sings, and pantomimes the universal endeavors of the lady to
capture the man. . . . It is something to see, this *A Star Is Born*.

(BOSLEY CROWTHER)

The New York Herald Tribune
It is fun to have her back on the screen again, reminiscing through
yesterday's songs in a long sequence, "Born in a Trunk," and
delivering new ones . . . in her direct, energetic style.

Time
Star is a massive effort . . . The producers assumed astonishing
risks. . . . The star, Judy Garland, was a 32-year-old has-been

"Born in a Trunk"

as infamous for temperament as she is famous for talent.

What's more, all the producers' worst dreams came true.
Day after day, while the high-priced help—including Judy's husband,
Producer Sid Luft—stood around waiting for the shooting to
start, Judy sulked in her dressing room. In the end *Star* took ten
months to make, cost $6,000,000. But after Judy had done her
worst in the dressing room, she did her best in front of the camera,
with the result that she gives what is just about the greatest
one-woman show in modern movie history.

With James Mason

With Tom Noonan and Charles Bickford

. . . Charles Bickford plays the big producer with vigor, and
Jack Carson is a howl as a press agent. Actor Mason, right to his
alcoholic end, glows with a seamless health and handsomeness. . . .

. . . As for Judy, she has never sung better. Harold Arlen and
Ira Gershwin have given her six good songs—among them
one unforgettable lump in the throat, "The Man That Got Away."

. . . An expert vaudeville performance was to be expected from
Judy; to find her a dramatic actress as well is the real surprise—
although perhaps it should not be.

. . . Judy Garland makes a stunning comeback. . . .

With James Mason and Charles Bickford

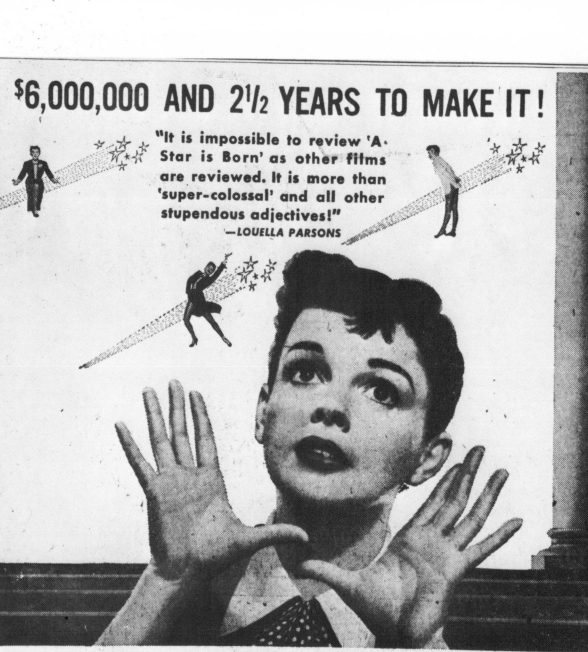

The cast of Pepe *as seen by the caricaturist Kroll: Greer Garson, Edward G. Robinson, Debbie Reynolds, Sammy Davis, Jr., Ernie Kovacs, Kim Novak, Bing Crosby, Shirley Jones, Dan Dailey. In background: Jack Lemmon, Jimmy Durante, Hedda Hopper, Maurice Chevalier. Cantinflas, the star, is shown fighting a bull, chatting with Cesar Romero, and showing off his great white stallion, Don Juan.*

Pepe

A Columbia Picture (1960)

Produced and directed by George Sidney
Screenplay by Dorothy Kingsley and Claude Binyon
Screen Story by Leonard Spigelgass and Sonya Levien
Based on a play by L. Bush-fekete
Associate Producer: Jacques Gelman
Music Supervision and background score: Johnny Green
Songs: "Faraway Part of Town," "That's How It Went, All Right"
    (Music, Andre Previn, Lyrics, Dory Langdon); "Pepe"
    (Music, Hans Wittstatt, Lyrics, Dory Langdon);
    "The Rumble" (Andre Previn); "Lovely Day" (Music,
    Augustin Lara, Spanish lyric, Maria Teresa Lara, English
    lyric, Dory Langdon)
Art Director: Ted Haworth
Cinematographer: Joe MacDonald
Editors: Viola Lawrence, Al Clark

COMMENTS

Judy sang "The Faraway Part of Town" for the soundtrack of
this all-star Columbia film, for a scene in which Dan Dailey
and Shirley Jones danced.

The song was nominated for an Academy Award.

Judgment at Nuremberg

A United Artists Release; a Roxlom Production (1961)

Produced and Directed by Stanley Kramer
Screenplay by Abby Mann (based on his television script)
Production Designer and Art Director: Rudolph Sternad
Music: Ernest Gold
Associate Producer: Philip Langner
Cinematographer: Ernest Laszlo
Editor: Fred Knudston

CAST

Spencer Tracy, Burt Lancaster, Richard Widmark, Marlene Dietrich,
Maximilian Schell, Judy Garland, Montgomery Clift,
William Shatner, Edward Binns, Kenneth McKenna,
Werner Klemperer, Alan Baxter, Torben Meyer, Roy Teal,
Martin Brandt, Virginia Christine, Ben Wright, Joseph Bernard,
John Wengraf, Karl Swenson, Howard Caine, Otto Waldis,
Olga Fabian, Sheila Bromley, Bernard Kates, Jana Taylor,
Paul Busch.

COMMENTS
Judgment at Nuremberg tells the story of Dan Haywood

With Richard Widmark and unidentified player

With Montgomery Clift

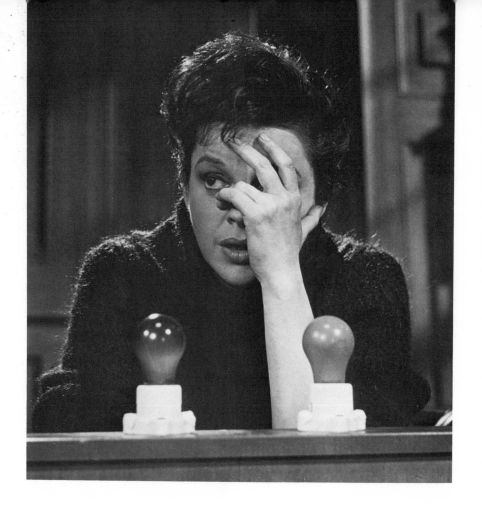

(Spencer Tracy), an American judge presiding at the Nuremberg trials. Three German judges are on trial, accused of destroying law and justice to support Hitler.

The proceedings reach a climax when a woman named Irene Hoffman (Judy Garland) is called to the stand. She testifies that a former friend, an elderly Jew, was falsely accused of being intimate with her (thereby "polluting the Aryan race") and then executed. The defense attorney Hans Rolfe (Maximilian Schell) tries to break her story and accuses her of distorting the truth. While under pressure, the distraught woman breaks into hysterical denials. Unable to bear any more, Ernest Janning (Burt Lancaster), one of the three German judges, interrupts the hearing and asks to make a statement.

Janning had remained silent throughout the trial but now voluntarily takes the stand and admits to being guilty of both ignoring and rationalizing the inhuman Nazi acts because he felt they were for the country's ultimate good.

For political reasons the military suggests quick and lenient action in the case but Haywood and his associate judges refuse to compromise and sentence the three to life imprisonment. Rolfe prophesises that they will be free in five years.

Judgment at Nuremberg was first performed on television's "Playhouse 90" in 1959. Claude Rains was Haywood, Paul Lukas was Janning, and Maximilian Schell was the lawyer for the defense (a role he recreated for the motion picture). George Roy Hill directed the TV production.

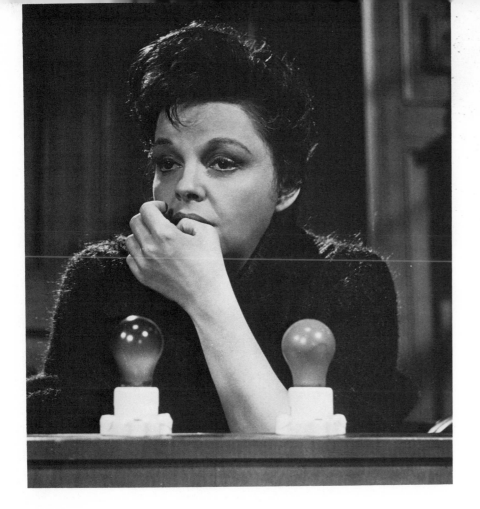

The film version was both a critical and financial success.
Judy sensitively etched a stunning portrait of a pathetic German
hausfrau torn between retaining personal happiness and security
and seeking justice at the Nuremberg trials.

It was a small but key role, and earned Judy another Oscar
nomination, this time as Best Supporting Actress.

This film and her successful concert and television appearances
precipitated a brief resurgence in her motion picture career.

With Spencer Tracy

Mewsette and admirer

Gay Purr-ee

A Warner Brothers Release; a UPA Production (1962)

Judy (who supplied the voice for Mewsette)

Hermione Gingold

Executive Producer: Henry G. Saperstein
Directed by Abe Leviton
Screenplay by Dorothy and Chuck Jones
Music by Harold Arlen and E. Y. Harburg
Music arranged and conducted by Mort Lindsay
Vocal arrangements by Joseph J. Lilley
Associate Producer: Lee Orgel
Photography: Roy Hutchcroft, Dan Miller, Jack Stevens and
    Duane Keegan
Art Director: Victor Haboush
Editor: Ted Baker

A full-length animated feature utilizing the voices of:
Judy Garland, Robert Goulet, Red Buttons, Hermione Gingold,
Paul Frees, Morey Amsterdam, Mel Blanc, Julie Bennett,
and Joan Gardner.

Robert Goulet

Red Buttons

COMMENTS

This was a UPA feature-length cartoon in which Judy was the
voice of the sexy, fun-loving kitten, Mewsette. The score included
six new Harold Arlen-E. Y. Harburg songs.

E. Y. HARBURG comments: Judy is still a fast learner. When
Harold Arlen and I worked with her on the score for *Gay Purr-ee,*
she sat down at the piano with Harold and began singing along.
She was almost a line ahead of him. She is so attuned, has such an
affinity for music and lyrics, you don't have to tell Judy anything.

What the critics said about
   GAY PURR-EE

Newsweek

The little cat who is the heroine of this improbable feature-length
animated cartoon is named Mewsette. She comes to the big city
(Purr-ee) where she meets the evil Meowrice, a shabby tabby if
ever there was one. He takes her to the Mewlon Rouge, and the
Felines-Bergère, and shows her Meowmartre, but he is a vile
cat-napper, and means to mail Mewsette off to some old fat cat in
Pittsburgh. (Why not the Cat's Kills, or Kitty Hawk, or Katonah,
or even Pussburgh?) But Meowrice is foiled by Mewsette's old swain
from the farm, and its ends purrfectly blissfully.

   The visual style is van Gogh out of Magoo. There are songs
with lines like "The chestnut, the willow, the colors of Utrillo,"
voiced with varying competence by Judy Garland and Robert Goulet.
There seems to be an effort to reach a hitherto undiscovered
audience—the fey four-year-old of recherché taste.

With Bruce Ritchey

A Child Is Waiting

A United Artists Release; a Stanley Kramer Production, (1962)

Produced by Stanley Kramer
Directed by John Cassavetes
Screenplay by Abby Mann (based on his television play)
Music by Ernest Gold
Associate Producer: Philip Langner
Photography: Joseph LaShelle
Editor: Gene Fowler, Jr.
Art Direction: Rudolph Sternad

CAST

Burt Lancaster, Judy Garland, Gena Rowlands, Steven Hill,
Bruce Ritchey, Gloria McGehee, Paul Stewart, Elizabeth Wilson,
Barbara Pepper, John Morley, June Walker, Mario Gallo,
Frederick Draper, Lawrence Tierney.

COMMENTS

The movie starred Burt Lancaster as Dr. Matthew Clark, the superintendent doctor of a state institution for mentally retarded children, and Judy Garland as Jean Hansen, a new music teacher on Clark's staff.

With Bruce Ritchey

Jean is anxious to give some meaning to her life, and she regards Clark's stern training methods with suspicion. She tries to shelter the children with her love. Twelve-year-old Reuben Widdicombe (Bruce Ritchey) is a borderline case, abandoned by his divorced parents. Jean becomes emotionally involved with him.

When Reuben stubbornly refuses to follow orders, Jean defies Clark by sending for Reuben's parents. Mrs. Widdicombe (Gena Rowlands) agrees with the doctor and decides not to see the boy. But as she is leaving the institution Reuben catches sight of her and chases her departing car. Emotionally upset by the incident, the boy runs away. When he is returned to the school the next morning, Jean, realizing her mistake, offers to resign.

Clark suggests that she remain on and continue her preparations for a Thanksgiving show in which all the children will perform. On the day of the show Reuben's father (Steven Hill) comes to transfer his son to a private school. When he hears Reuben haltingly recite a poem and then respond to the audience's applause, he better understands his son's desperate need to achieve something for himself.

This was a disturbingly realistic story of the problems of the mentally retarded and their families. Judy's sensitivity and warmth were perfect for her role as the music teacher who felt love would solve the children's problems. It was her best straight dramatic performance.

Except for Bruce Ritchey, the children in the film were patients at the Pacific State Hospital in Pomona, California. *A Child Is*

With Burt Lancaster

Waiting was originally a 1957 teleplay. On television it starred
Pat Hingle, Mary Fickett and Marian Seldes and was directed by
Vincent Donahue.

The theme of *A Child Is Waiting* was too strong for mass appeal,
and, although most critics praised the movie, and the actors, it
was not considered a box-office success.

What the critics said about
A CHILD IS WAITING

The New York Times
Some painful but compelling instruction on how to adjust
emotionally to the sometimes calamitous problem of the mentally
retarded child is conveyed with courageous candor and dramatic
simplicity. . . .

Time
. . . The film is bone honest and at moments mortally moving.
Garland is good.

Saturday Review
Wonderful . . . is the way Judy Garland and Burt Lancaster work
along with the children. Miss Garland and Lancaster radiate a
warmth so genuine that one is certain that the children are
responding directly to them, not merely following some vaguely
comprehended script.

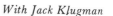
With Jack Klugman

I Could Go On Singing

A United Artists Release; a Barbican Production (1962)

Produced by Stuart Millar and Lawrence Turman
Directed by Ronald Neame
Screenplay by Mayo Simon
Story by Robert Dozier
Music Supervision: Saul Chaplin
Title Song by Harold Arlen and E. Y. Harburg
Associate Producer: Dennis Holt
Photography: Arthur Ibbetson
Editor: John Shirley
Art Direction: Wilfred Shingleton

With Dirk Bogarde

With Gregory Phillips and classmates

CAST
Judy Garland, Dirk Bogarde, Jack Klugman, Gregory Phillips, Aline MacMahon, Pauline Jameson, Jeremy Burnham, Russell Waters, Gerald Sim, Leon Cortez.

COMMENTS
Judy's last picture to date presented her in a role quite similar to her real-life personality, that of a successful concert singer tortured by emotional and personal problems.

The picture, filmed in England, managed to capture the excitement of her concert appearances, although the story line was rather trite.

As always, Judy was believable, but the strain of her personal problems was taking its toll on her physical appearance on screen.

What the critics said about
   I COULD GO ON SINGING

Variety
A femme *Jolson Story* . . . A soulful performance is etched by Miss Garland, who gives more than she gets from the script.

The New York Times
Considering what Judy Garland has done in movies over the years and how many of her fans still love her, no matter what she does, it is sad to have to say that the little lady is not at the top of her form in her new film, *I Could Go On Singing*.
                                          (BOSLEY CROWTHER)

The New York Post
I Could Go On Singing . . . is a showcase for Judy Garland's latter-day singing . . . and emoting. There are good scenes of

With Dirk Bogarde

England . . . also good personal scenes, with steam provided by Judy Garland and ice courtesy of Dirk Bogarde. As for the story, it's soppy. . . . The entertainment rests solely and heavily on the very theatrical shoulders of Judy Garland. (ARCHER WINSTEN)

The New York Herald Tribune
Either you are or you aren't—a Judy Garland fan that is. And if you aren't, forget about her new movie, *I Could Go On Singing*, and leave the discussion to us devotees.

You'll see her in close-up . . . in beautiful, glowing Technicolor and striking staging in a vibrant, vital performance that gets to the essence of her mystique as a superb entertainer. Miss Garland is—as always—real, the voice throbbing, the eyes aglow, the delicate features yielding to the demands of the years—the legs still long and lovely. Certainly the role of a top-rank singer beset by the loneliness and emotional hungers of her personal life is not an alien one to her. . . . (JUDITH CRIST)

The New York Daily News
3 stars. . . . Judy Garland is back on screen in a role that might have been custom-tailored for her particular talents. A new song, "I Could Go on Singing," provides her with a little clowning, a chance to be gay, a time for wistfulness, an occasion for tears. She and Dirk Bogarde play wonderfully well together, even though the script itself insists on their being mismatched. . . .

(DOROTHY MASTERS)

Belting out "I Could Go on Singing"

In Broadway Melody of 1938

Songs from Judy's Films

FILM	SONGS
PIGSKIN PARADE	"Balboa"
BROADWAY MELODY OF 1938	"(Dear Mr. Gable) You Made Me Love You,"
	"Everybody Sing," "Yours and Mine"
THOROUGHBREDS DON'T CRY	"Got a Pair of New Shoes"
LISTEN, DARLING	"On a Bumpy Road to Love"
LOVE FINDS ANDY HARDY	"Zing Went the Strings of My Heart"
THE WIZARD OF OZ	"Over the Rainbow," "We're Off to See the Wizard"
BABES IN ARMS	"I Cried for You," "I'm Just Wild About Harry," "God's Country"
STRIKE UP THE BAND	"My Wonderful One," "Our Love Affair"

LITTLE NELLY KELLY	"It's a Great Day for the Irish"
BABES ON BROADWAY	"How About You?"
FOR ME AND MY GAL	"For Me and My Gal" "When You Wore a Tulip," "After You've Gone"
GIRL CRAZY	"Embraceable You," "Biding My Time," "But Not for Me," "I've Got Rhythm"
THOUSANDS CHEER	"The Joint Is Really Jumping Down at Carnegie Hall"
MEET ME IN ST. LOUIS	"The Trolley Song," "The Boy Next Door," "Have Yourself a Merry Little Christmas" "Skip to My Lou"
THE HARVEY GIRLS	"On the Atchison, Topeka and Santa Fe"
TILL THE CLOUDS ROLL BY	"Who," "Look for the Silver Lining"
THE PIRATE	"Love of My Life," "Be a Clown," "Mack the Black"

With Ray Bolger in The Wizard of Oz

In For Me and My Gal

EASTER PARADE	"Better Luck Next Time," "A Couple of Swells"
WORDS AND MUSIC	"I Wish I Were in Love Again," "Johnny One Note"
IN THE GOOD OLD SUMMERTIME	"I Don't Care," "Play That Barbershop Chord"
SUMMER STOCK	"Get Happy," "Happy Harvest"
A STAR IS BORN	"The Man That Got Away," "Born in a Trunk," "It's a New World" "Swanee"
PEPE	"Faraway Part of Town"
I COULD GO ON SINGING	"I Could Go on Singing," "Hello, Bluebird"

At the Palace Theatre, 1951

JUDY: *In Concert*

Although Judy Garland came to prominence and gained popularity in films (and she herself has said that M-G-M has been the greatest single influence in her career), for the past eighteen years Judy's professional life has been primarily in concerts and television.

Whether a Garland fan or not, anyone who has seen and heard Judy Garland perform in concert is overpowered by her uncanny ability to project her personality and her feeling for a song. Many have said "She sings into the hearts of people" and "It's as if she's singing just to me" or "I feel like I'm up there with her."

Others may entertain; Judy Garland captures and enchants an audience.

Judy had literally grown up on stage and was a vaudeville veteran at thirteen, when she signed for films. In the ensuing years, M-G-M sent her and Mickey Rooney on countless personal appearance tours to perform in stage shows.

While under contract to M-G-M, Judy made her first formal concert appearance in July, 1943, at the Robin Hood Dell in Philadelphia. A capacity crowd heard her sing songs from her films and a selection of Gershwin tunes. The studio claimed that 15,000 people had to be turned away. That same year Judy made an extensive USO tour.

With James Stewart, at the closing of the 1951 Palace engagement

Although her personal appearance tours became less frequent in the 40's, she was well known in Hollywood as an eager and willing performer at benefits and parties.

When her movie career seemed at a forced end in 1950, Judy Garland turned to stage performing for financial and emotional rewards. Both came quickly.

In 1951, earning $20,000 a week, she was a smash hit at the London Palladium and carried her success across the Atlantic to New York's Palace Theatre.

Judy enjoyed another successful run at the Palace in 1956, and in May, 1959, she played a one-week benefit engagement at New York's Metropolitan Opera House. (Featured in the first half of her shows at the Palace and the Met was a talented but relatively unknown comedian, Alan King.)

Perhaps Judy's most resounding success to date occurred in 1961, when she gave her now legendary concert at Carnegie Hall, which was recorded on the scene, and provided her with her most successful record album, "Judy at Carnegie Hall."

Judy Garland has given countless successful concerts throughout the world since then, and continues to be one of the biggest "in person" box-office draws.

What the critics said about
JUDY AT THE PALACE (1951)

The New York Daily News (October 30, 1951)
The revival of the two-a-day at the Palace Theatre offers a good

enough bill with a remarkably engaging performance by
Judy Garland, and the professional sentimentalists would have
you believe that this successful booking presages the revival of
vaudeville. The sentimentalists are wrong, as usual. Vaudeville still is
dead and it is going to remain dead.

The live one is Miss Garland, who deserves all the success she
is having because she works so hard to earn it. She is on the stage
for the entire last half of the bill (which is not real vaudeville at
all, but a personal appearance). She has three sets of costumes,
including her famous tramp getup, and she sings as hard and as long
as she can. She gets chummy with the audience, with conductor
Max Meth in the pit and with pianist-composer Hugh Martin—
whose Steinway is placed about as far upstage as it can be moved
without knocking out a wall, in order that Miss Garland may
have the forestage to herself.

Miss Garland is up there to sing, and she sings. There is no
holding back, and this generosity on the part of a performer is not
usual in these days of personal appearances. Her songs include, of
course, a medley of old two-a-day favorites like Sophie Tucker's
"Some of These Days" and Nora Bayes' "Shine On, Harvest Moon."
Included in this popular melange is an Al Jolson number, although
Jolson never played the Palace. The high moment in the
Garland performance is carefully timed and staged—an enchanting
rendition of "Over the Rainbow" with Judy incongruously clad
in her tramp suit and sitting dirty-faced on the stage with her legs
hanging over the orchestra pit.

The audience, fed up with simpering personal appearances, is
enormously enthusiastic. It has found a friend in Judy and it
responds by being her friend. The night I caught the Palace bill an
elderly juvenile named Montgomery Clift, squiring a nice-looking
and well-behaved girl named Taylor or something, was unable to
limit his applause to mere handclapping. He tried repeatedly to
stomp his feet through the floor, and, since he was in the first row
on the center aisle, he almost scared the wits out of the orchestra
leader, Mr. Meth, the first time he tried it. I think Mr. Clift
must have wanted Miss Garland to notice him, if she hadn't before....
(JOHN CHAPMAN)

Variety (February 27, 1952)
Judy Garland's closing performance at the Palace, N. Y.,
Sunday (24) will remain one of the more memorable experiences
in the history of a two-a-day. A loaded house in a sentimental
mood sent Judy off stage in tears with the mass singing of
"Auld Lang Syne." It was one of the warmest tributes ever given a
headliner in New York.

Miss Garland's Palace run made show business history firstly by
proving that two-a-day can be a top box-office medium and that
the Palace name is still an important entertainment landmark.
It needed a Judy Garland to prove that vaudeville can still be sold
at $4.80 and that a performer of Miss Garland's magnitude can
run indefinitely on that basis. It's generally conceded that
Miss Garland could have remained another 19 weeks had she so

With Jerry Lewis in Las Vegas, 1957

desired. The bill grossed approximately $750,000 in that run of which $50,000 came the final week with 11 performances. It's more than was ever grossed by any other vaude bill.

The Sunday night show presented a peculiar parlay of circumstances. In the first place more than 50% of the house had seen the show before. House contained many black ties and the audience included Joe Louis, Phil Silvers, Barry Gray, Faye Emerson and Skitch Henderson, Shelley Winters, Ben Blue. Lauritz Melchior came to observe just how to operate during his first N. Y. vaude engagement.

Melchior drew the slyest laugh of the evening. When called upon on stage by Miss Garland, the former Metopera Wagnerian tenor recalled that he used to work a house a few blocks down the street. He left that house with a Bing, and said he "hoped to go over here with a bang." Melchior, of course, was referring to the fact that he had some difficulties with Rudolf Bing, Met's general manager.

However, the prevailing sentiment seemed to be lachrymose. After the audience got through cheering Miss Garland, both

With Frank Sinatra at the Cocoanut Grove, 1958

At Carnegie Hall, 1961

manually and vocally, she did her first encore, "Over the Rainbow"
in her tramp costume used in "Couple of Swells." There were
moments when tears came to Miss Garland during its rendition.
The effect was similar on many members of the audience.
Speeches and three extra numbers didn't suffice. The crowd just
didn't move, although most knew that she had already done three
numbers more than in her usual shows. There were requests
from all over the house. A voice in the direction of her manager-
fiancé Sid Luft apparently suggested that the audience sing
to her. Miss Garland took up that suggestion, stood back and
waited. In short order, maestro Jack Cathcart maestroed
"Auld Lang Syne." Halfway through the number Melchior stood
up, and the rest of the house followed suit. It had sufficient
emotional wallop to bring tears.

Miss Garland has set a pattern that will be hard for anybody to
follow. At her opening, the public seemed to sense that she
needed to make good on this engagement if her career was to
continue. Theatregoers knew that she was a sick kid, and there was
a collective feeling that they would give her the security she
needed. Her public may well have contributed considerable therapy
to her physical and mental comeback. Her professional status
was never in doubt.

What the critics said about
JUDY AT THE PALACE (1956)

The New York Times
Nothing really important seems to have happened since Judy Garland was last here five years ago. . . .

As on her previous visit, she takes over the second half of the program with the songs she sings as though she were composing them on the spot. . . .

A song has not really been sung until Judy pulls herself together and belts it through the theatre. (BROOKS ATKINSON)

What the critics said about
JUDY AT CARNEGIE HALL

The New York Herald Tribune (April 24, 1961)
There was an extra bonus at Carnegie Hall last night.
Judy Garland sang.

She didn't have to, as far as the fans jamming the walls of the hall were concerned. The very overture, involving "The Trolley Song" and "Over the Rainbow," was drowned in applause and when Miss Garland appeared she got a standing ovation that

Carnegie Hall, 1961

went on and on and on and on. Hers was a personal triumph
right there. And then she sang.

And she sang, let it be reported, as she hasn't in years—not at
the Palace and not at the Met; she sang with all the heart that has
been her hallmark, but added to it is a happy self-confidence
that gives new quality and depth to her performance. It's a
performance that deserves all the pre-commitment her very
name evokes.

There's no blatant banking on nostalgia, even though all her
standards are in the program, from "When You're Smiling" right
down to "Chicago." But the tuxed-and-chorus boys and smudge-
faced-tramp routines have been set aside; there's only some joyous
heel-kicking onstage, the donning of a top hat for "Swanee"
and some self-derogating chit-chat in Bankheadish tones and
good humor.

But it's a satisfying solo performance. For Judy Garland is a
gal who can belt it out right over the brassiest band and belt it
strong and true. And she can sit down with the pianist and whisper
it a little and get that heart-pulling quaver on just the right notes.
And she can swing it out with a jazz octet with a purity of
style and true tempo that verges on the classic.

This is a stylish, poised Miss Garland, slim-legged and big
bosomed, chic in a black sheath and blue jeweled mandarin jacket
for the first half of the program and black toreador pants and
sequined top for the second. She also has a stylish hairdo that
collapses in no time at all with all her characteristic brushing-back
of her bangs and her athletic enthusiasm in the depths of song.

It is a gay Miss Garland and a sure one—with plenty of reason for her new self assurance.

Her ingenuous warmth dominates the evening, but there is neither coyness nor girly-girlishness in her approach. She can jazz up "Puttin' on the Ritz" with a fine flair, bring down the walls with "Come Rain or Come Shine" and bring a raucous hall to reverent silence with "I Can't Give You Anything But Love, Baby."

Well, I can't give you anything but raves, Miss Garland. And it's a pleasure to note a repeat concert is scheduled for May 21. (JUDITH CRIST)

What the Critics said about
JUDY AT THE PALACE (1967)

The New York Times (August 1, 1967)
Judy Garland returned to the Palace last night like some raffish, sequin-sprinkled female Lazarus. That magnetic talent is alive once again in New York, and so is one of the most remarkable personalities of the contemporary entertainment scene. That the voice—as of last night's performance, anyway—is now a memory seems almost beside the point.

The show that will occupy the Palace for the next four weeks

is a top-notch vaudeville presentation, touched by the pathos of
real-life soap opera.

Miss Garland is headlining a fine bill that includes
Jackie Vernon, the dead-pan night-club comic who is shaped like
an inverted bowling pin; John Bubbles, the old soft shoe and tap
man, and Francis Brunn, an incredible juggler (or a juggler of
incredible abilities).

It is, however, her show, and although she does not come on until
the second half, her presence dominates the proceedings from
the first note of the overture. That is, her presence and those sad
and forlorn tales of her personal life that we all know so well and

At the Palace, 1967

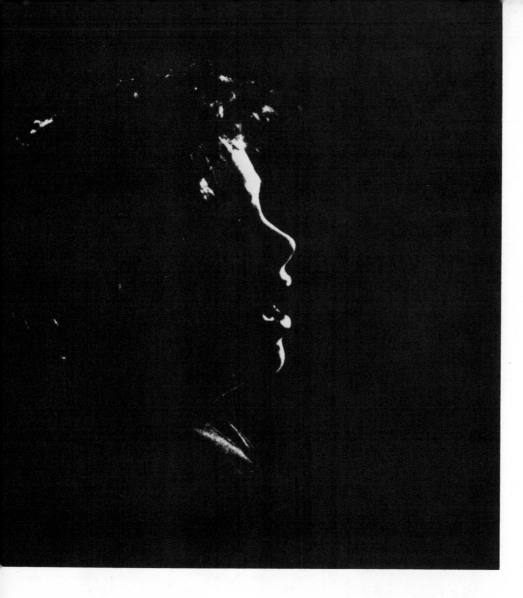

that inevitably color our reaction to her actual performances for better and for worse.

Aside from the problems with her voice—and, let's face it, there are thousands of singers with voices, if that's all you want—Miss Garland was in fine fettle last night. All the Garland favorites were brought out—"The Man That Got Away," "What Now My Love," "Rockabye My Baby," "Chicago" and countless others.

Giving their mother unbilled support were Lorna and Joey Luft, 14 and 12, respectively. That they are not show business-trained was only too obvious as they joined Miss Garland and Mr. Bubbles in a rather haphazard run-through of "Me and My Shadow." Curiously, this very lack of professionalism added a sweet, if sometimes embarrassing, dimension to the show.

Miss Luft is a tall little girl, on the brink of turning into a very pretty woman. Her younger brother, who whacked away at the drums for a few moments, is like anybody's little brother, performing in the living room.

This kind of amateur, *en famille* performance can be very winning in the intimacy of a TV screen, but it doesn't quite work on the huge Palace stage. It is vaudeville soap opera. . . .

(Vincent Canby)

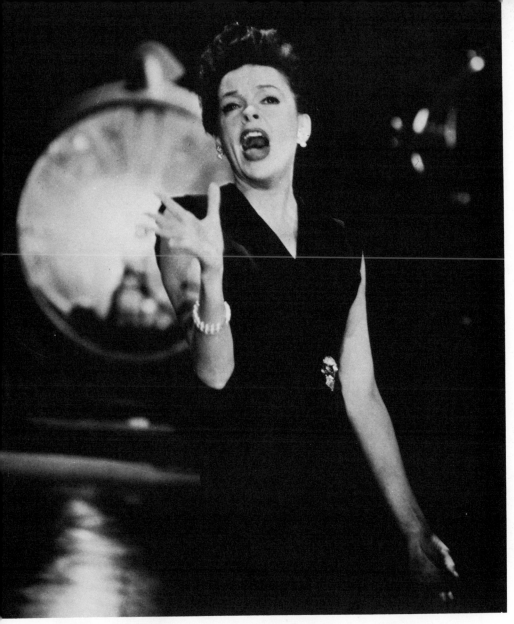

JUDY: *On Television*

Judy Garland is a very special and unique star. She is one of the few to excel in all media of show business. She is a *performer* in addition to being an accomplished actress-singer-dancer, with a masterful flair for comedy. She possesses personality and warmth, the keys for television success.

And the television specials in which Judy starred were very successful indeed. In 1955, she made her television debut with a spectacular for the Ford Motor Company, "The Ford Star Jubilee."

After Judy's highly-acclaimed return to concerts and films in the early 60's, CBS presented "The Judy Garland Show," a one-hour special teaming her with her friends Frank Sinatra and Dean Martin. This highly-rated and well-accepted program led to additional specials and a series for CBS in 1963.

Her weekly one-hour musical-variety series, "The Judy Garland Show," premiered in September, 1963. Judy was hostess to some of the top names in show business, including Lena Horne, Ethel Merman, Peggy Lee, and, of course, Mickey Rooney. Barbra Streisand made a memorable appearance on one of Judy's shows. It was instrumental in Barbra's push to stardom, and soon after, she signed for a series of specials of her own for CBS.

Unfortunately, as a musical variety program which called for Judy to serve as sort of a female Garry Moore, the show was not well received, either critically or as far as ratings went. It was also up against the stiffest competition, NBC's "Bonanza," then at the peak of its unprecedented popularity.

When, for the last few programs of her series, she took center stage and spent the entire hour in concert, the show came alive and critics did an about-face. But it was too late. High production costs and low ratings led to Judy's announcement that she would not continue the show after the 26th episode.

The network was bombarded with cards, letters and telegrams. Loyal Garland fans wanted the Rainbow Girl to continue on television.

She remains one of the most highly sought-after guest stars for leading television shows, and in the unpredictable world of TV, it is not unlikely that she will return as a regular attraction.

With Barbra Streisand

With Jack Paar

*With daughter Liza Minnelli
and Ed Sullivan*

What the critics said about
THE FORD STAR JUBILEE

The Special on which Judy made
her television debut in 1955

The New York Herald Tribune
Although burdened with laryngitis, Judy Garland demonstrated on
television Saturday night . . . that she is still a tremendous figure
in the realm of show business. The occasion was her TV debut on
the opening of "The Ford Star Jubilee," a live 90-minute
monthly color series. . . .

. . . She delivered [songs] with a unique, impish charm and that
unmistakable throb in her voice.

. . . The pity of it was that the production failed to match her
casual, lighthearted style. It opened on a pretentious note and there-
after little was done to enhance her very special qualities. . . . (M.T.)

New York World-Telegram & Sun
Anyone who has ever watched Judy Garland in person, walk out
on a stage and sing, who has watched her immediately and

*With Dean Martin and
Frank Sinatra*

magically establish her unique rapport with the audience, knows
he has seen someone who has become a living legend of her day.

(MARGARET McMANUS)

What the critics said about
THE JUDY GARLAND SHOW

A Special starring Judy, Frank Sinatra
and Dean Martin, aired in February, 1962

The New York Times
Judy Garland held television in the palm of her hands last night.
In her first video appearance in six years the singer carried on the
music hall tradition of Al Jolson and other greats; she sang
her heart out with emotion, energy and magnetism.
    . . . Miss Garland was supported by two gentlemen, Frank Sinatra
and Dean Martin, who happen to be modern exponents of the
oft-forgotton law that there is more to a song than just singing it;
the number also must be put across. That was accomplished by
all three on easily the most melodic hour of several TV seasons.
    Miss Garland's program . . . was sublimely content to let

With Ethel Merman

With Peggy Lee

With Ray Bolger

With Lena Horne

Miss Garland and her colleagues speak for themselves. Virtually the entire sixty minutes were pure song, with an absolute minimum of superfluous chitchat.

. . . Miss Garland's total involvement and her passionate sincerity were contagious.

. . . It was the spell that the occasional performer can weave in his or her own way and everyone, without knowing precisely why, is glad to savor. Miss Garland is to be numbered among the theatre's chosen few. . . . (JACK GOULD)

What the critics said about
THE JUDY GARLAND SHOW

The premiere show of Miss Garland's
CBS Series, September 29, 1963

The New York Times
What should never happen to Judy Garland did last evening in the premiere of her weekly program over the Columbia

With Mickey Rooney

Broadcasting System. The busybodies got so in the way that the singer never had a chance to sing out as only she can. To call the hour a grievous disappointment would be to miss the point. It was an absolute mystery.

. . . The thinking of CBS executives apparently was to develop a "new" Judy, one who would indulge in light banter and make way for suitable guests to share the weekly tasks. By such tactics it was presumably thought that Miss Garland could be shielded from burning herself out musically.

. . . She was a prisoner of her production.

. . . Those telephones on the 20th floor of CBS's home encampment should buzz this morning with but one directive to Hollywood. Free Judy! (JACK GOULD)

JUDY: *Her Life in Headlines*

1939   1939   1940

Juvenile Stars Draw 15,000 to the Capitol

40 Policemen Handle Line at 'Wizard of Oz' Opening

The personal appearances of Mickey Rooney and Judy Garland at the premiere of the motion picture "The Wizard of Oz" drew 15,-000 persons yesterday morning to the Capitol Theater. Forty policemen were required to handle a line five and six deep that stretched from the box office at Broadway and Fifty-first Street all the way around the block, hampering pedestrian traffic on Broadway, Eighth Avenue and Fiftieth and Fifty-first Streets.

The crowd, composed chiefly of children in their 'teens, started to assemble at 5:30 a. m. By 8 a. m., when the box office opened, there were 10,000 waiting to enter the theater, which seats 5,400. At 9:10 a. m., two hours before the juvenile stars were to appear, the standees were estimated by police

Judy Garland Becomes Star In New Film

HOLLYWOOD, Oct. 11.—(AP)—Judy Garland woke up today an established movie star. Two things proved it.

First, her footprints were in the cement before Grauman's Chinese Theatre, along with those of three-score of filmdom's greatest.

Second, critics were unanimous and lavish in the acclaim of "Babes In Arms," her co-starring musical with Mickey Rooney, premiered last night. Coming on top of her triumph in "The Wizard of Oz," it puts the petite Judy definitely in the front rank of celluliod celebrities.

It's a story of the offspring of

Rooney Tops Movie Stars

HOLLYWOOD, Dec. 27 (AP).—Mickey Rooney heads the 10 biggest money-making movie stars for 1940 as selected by the Motion Picture Herald, a trade publication. His nearest feminine competitor is Bette Davis, in ninth position.

Judy Garland, in 10th place, is the only other actress on the list.

Spencer Tracy placed second to Rooney, while following in order came Clark Gable, Gene Autry, Tyrone Power, James Cagney, Bing Crosby and Wallace Beery.

Selection of Autry, the sing-

1940   1940

Judy Garland to Get $680,000 in 7 Years

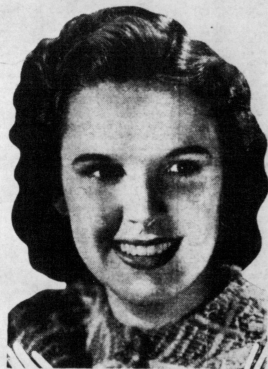

Judy Garland

Los Angeles, Sept. 26 (AP).—Ever wonder what Judy Garland is paid for looking so cute and singing so prettily? Here are the figures, contained in her new contract filed in Superior Court today: $2,000 a week for the next three years, $2,500 for the two years following, $3,000 for the last two years — a total of $680,000. She is guaranteed 40 weeks' work each year.

Judy Garland To Wed Rose

Star Will Celebrate Birthday Tomorrow

HOLLYWOOD, June 9.—(AP)—Judy Garland and Dave Rose became engaged recently and will make it "official" on Judy's birthday tomorrow, June 10.

Most movie-goers are familiar with the voice and face of the 18-year-old singer from Grand Rapids, Minn.

About Rose, the average fan knows little except that he is the former husband of Comedienne Martha Raye and is described vaguely as an orchestra leader or songwriter.

Here are some more facts about David Daniel Rose, 30, gleaned while watching him at work at the Mutual Broadcasting Studio the other day:

He is blond but deeply tanned from frequent visits to the beach. He is of medium height, has brown hair, dresses neatly and is quiet-spoken. The girls might call him "not handsome, but attractive."

Dorothy Lamour, Jeanette Mac-

First Love Scene Gets Her Jittery

Judy Garland Finds It Difficult to Grow Up in Film Business

"It isn't that I expected my fist real love scene to be glamorous—but I did think that maybe I could wear some kind of an evening gown, or have my hair done —well—something special."

So remarks Judy Garland, apropos of her first love scene as a solo star. She plays it opposite Douglas McPhail in "Little Nellie Kelly," the filmization of George M. Cohan's stage play, now at Loew's Metropolitan Theater.

But, instead of the evning gown, she played it in blue and white checked gingham, and with her hair caught at the nape of her neck in a flat red bow.

"I was terribly nervous," she says, "and, when they wanted me to look at the 'rushes' of the scene

JUDY GARLAND IN HOSPITAL

Film Actress Will Have Physical Checkup in Boston Institution

BOSTON, May 29 (UP)—Judy Garland, film actress, arrived here by train from Hollywood today and entered a hospital for a physical checkup.

Her manager, Carlton Alsop, said the checkup would be conducted by Dr. George W. Thorn, physician-in-chief at Peter Bent Brigham hospital and a Harvard Medical School professor. She decided to come East after she was removed from her role in the film version of "Annie Get Your Gun."

Miss Garland will visit New York on leaving the hospital and then perhaps accept an offer to appear in London.

JUDY GARLAND OUT OF THE 'ANNIE' FILM

Actress Suspended by Metro After Quitting Musical Role —Picture Is Half Done

By THOMAS F. BRADY
Special to THE NEW YORK TIMES.

HOLLYWOOD, Calif., May 10— Production of "Annie Get Your Gun" was halted today at Metro-Goldwyn-Mayer because Judy Garland, star of the film, walked out at lunch time and did not return. A studio statement declared: "Miss Garland refused to report on the set of "Annie Get Your Gun" after lunch today and has been suspended from salary by the studio. There are no plans for replacing her."

The actress was not available for comment, but Arthur Freed, producer of the film, said that she had repeatedly been late for work during the making of the picture, which has been before the cameras since April 4 and is now about half

'REBELLION' ENDS FOR JUDY GARLAND

Star Notifies Metro of Return After 12-Week Walkout From Cast of 'Annie'

By THOMAS F. BRADY
Special to THE NEW YORK TIMES.

HOLLYWOOD, Calif., July 31— Judy Garland, who was suspended from salary by Metro-Goldwyn-Mayer on May 10 for walking out on her assignment, "Annie Get Your Gun," has notified Metro executives that she will return to the studio this week, it was announced.

After her rebellion, Miss Garland went to Boston for a "rest cure" in a sanitarium, and the studio put her on "part salary" status.

Although she is completely well, she will not return to the cast of "Annie Get Your Gun," according to Metro. Betty Hutton will take over the "Annie" role, on loan-out from Paramount, and Miss Garland is expected to make her next screen appearance in "Summer Stock," which will go before the cameras in the fall with Gene

No Plans at M-G-M For Judy Garland

No Films for Her, Not Even a Conference, Studio Says

HOLLYWOOD, June 21 (UP).— Judy Garland may not make any more pictures for Metro-Goldwyn-Mayer, a studio spokesman said today.

Miss Garland rested at home with a bandage on her neck while Jane Powell tried out for the part in "Royal Wedding" over which Miss Garland cut her throat slightly with the edge of a broken drinking glass Monday night. The action took place after she found out she had been taken off the picture.

"Jane Powell is the Number One candidate to replace Judy," said Arthur Freed, producer of the movie. "Jane is trying out the songs right now on a rehearsal stage. e hope Judy does come back to make movies, but we can't say positively."

An M-G-M spokesman added that wheth the now nervous singer will ever face a camera again "remains to be seen." "No

Judy's Records At N. Y. Palace: 19 Weeks, 750G

Judy Garland winds up the Palace, the Broadway theatre's first attempt at two-a-day in 20 years, this Sunday (24) by shattering the house's record for longevity and grosses. Miss Garland will complete 19 weeks with an estimated $750,000. Palace Theatre execs feel she could have gone another 19 weeks just as easily. Ticket sales were very strong when announcement of the closing was made and zoomed to sellout propositions since.

Miss Garland's final stanza is expected to hit around $54,000 or over, her highest in the run. Last week, the theatre did $43,500. House is sold out on the last week and the final count will be determined by the number of standees permitted under the fire laws. Previous high was scored New Year's week, $53,000.

Miss Garland averaged around $15,000 weekly for her own share. She headed the package and paid the surrounding talent headed by

Judy Garland Made Show Biz History In Many Ways During Her Palace Run

Judy Garland's closing performance at the Palace, N. Y., Sunday (24) will remain one of the more memorable experiences in the history of two-a-day. A loaded house in a sentimental mood sent Judy off stage in tears with the mass singing of "Auld Lang Syne." It was one of the warmest tributes ever given a headliner in New York.

Miss Garland's Palace run made show business history firstly by proving that two-a-day can be a top boxoffice medium and that the Palace name is still an important entertainment landmark. It needed a Judy Garland to prove that vaudeville can still be sold at $4.80 and that a performer of Miss Garland's magnitude can run indefinitely on that basis. It's generally conceded that Miss Garland could have remained another 19 weeks had she so desired. The bill grossed approximately $750,-000 in that run of which $50,000 came the final week with 11 performances. It's more than was ever grossed by any other vaude

However, the prevailing sentiment seemed to be lachrymose. After the audience got through cheering Miss Garland, both manually and vocally, she did her first encore, "Over the Rainbow" in her tramp costume used in "Couple of Swells." There were moments when tears came to Miss Garland during its rendition. The effect was similar on many members of the audience. Speeches and three extra numbers didn't suffice. The crowd just didn't move, although most knew that she had already done three numbers more than in her usual shows. There were requests from all over the house. A voice in the direction of her manager-fiance Sid Luft apparently suggested that the audience sing to her. Miss Garland took up that suggestion, stood back and waited. In short order, maestro Jack Cathcart maestroed "Auld Lang Syne." Halfway through the number Melchior stood up, and the rest of the house followed suit. It had sufficient emotional wallop to bring

Judy Garland, Sid Luft To Be Married After All

NASSAU, Bahamas, March 21 (AP).—Actress Judy Garland and her business manager, Sid Luft, said today they are planning to get married after all. They arrived by plane from Palm Beach, Fla., for the Bahamas Country Club amateur invitation best ball golf tournament tomorrow.

Miss Garland said at Palm Beach March 6 that she did not plan to marry Mr. Luft because her final divorce decree from Ben Vincente Minelli, film director, wasn't due until today.

Today they agreed they intend to marry but did not know where or when. They are staying here until Monday.

[Miss Garland previously was married to David Rose, composer, from July, 1941, to June, 1945. A week after her divorce from Mr. Rose she was married to Mr. Minelli. Mr. Luft, a former test pilot, was married previously to actress Lynn Bari. They were married in 1943 and divorced in 1950.]

STAR TO PERFORM AS SHOW IS BORN

Judy Garland Will Appear on Premiere of 'Ford Jubilee' Sept. 24 Over C.B.S.-TV

By VAL ADAMS

Judy Garland will star on the première of the "Ford Star Jubilee" program on Saturday, Sept. 24, from 9:30 to 11 P. M. over the Columbia Broadcasting System television network.

Sid Luft, the singer's husband, will produce the program, which will be televised in color from Hollywood, Calif.

In making the announcement, C. B. S. did not say who would appear with Miss Garland or what the format would be. But an executive for the Music Corporation of America, the talent agency representing the singer, said her TV show would be similar to the stage show in which Miss Garland is touring on the West Coast.

The troupe, which includes

Her Comeback Credited to Him

Judy Garland Cites Cruelty, Sues Sid Luft for Divorce

SANTA MONICA, Calif., Feb. 3 (AP).—Actress Judy Garland filed suit for divorce today from actor's agent Sid Luft. She alleged extreme cruelty.

Miss Garland asked the court to make an equitable division of community property. She requested custody of the couple's children, Lorma, three, and Joseph, ten months old. The couple was married June 8, 1952.

Finds His Wife Gone

[Mr. Luft was reported to have returned to their Holmby Hills home at 6:45 p. m. to find Miss Garland and their children gone. He said he had no idea why they were absent until the United Press informed him of the divorce suit. "This is baloney," he said. "She left no note or anything. I just got home and haven't even looked around to see if he rclothes are gone. We didn't have any fight. This is a blow to me. The only reason I can see is that Judy hasn't been

dence the singer needed after her M.-G.-M. contract was severed. He put together a show starring his wife and took it to London's Palladium. The Londoners adored her and Mr. Luft presented her in a record breaking engagement at the Palace, in New York.

After her stage successes, Mr. Luft arranged a deal with Warner Brothers for him to produce a musical remake of "A Star Is Born," starring his wife.

In September, Mr. Luft starred Miss Garland in her television debut on Ford Star Jubilee. She was reported to have earned $100,000 for the appearance, with his fee as producer $10,000.

Mr. Luft, who was also a film writer before his marriage to Miss Garland, was often in court over money troubles with a former wife, actress Lynn Bari. She had sued him for nonsupport of their son, John.

Miss Garland, who is thirty-

LUFT'S LIEBE LOST: Charging extreme cruelty, songstress Judy Garland filed suit for divorce against producer Sid Luft, her third husband, in Santa Monica late yesterday. They're shown together at recent premiere of her film, "A Star Is Born."

Marie Torre Verdict:
10 Days for Contempt
Columnist Is Free Pending Appeal On Issue Involving News Source

By Milton Lewis

Marie Torre, TV-radio columnist for the New York Herald Tribune, we- formally held in criminal contempt of court yesterday and sentenced by a Federal judge to ten days in prison for steadfastly refusing to reveal the source of an item she printed about Judy Garland.

However, because Federal appellate courts have never ruled on this "substantial question of law," Judge Sylvester J. Ryan—who last month referred to Miss Torre as the "Joan of Arc of her profession"—released her in her own recognizance pending appeal.

A notice of appeal from Judge Ryan's ruling in United States District Court was filed immediately. Argument on the appeal will be heard in the United States Court of Appeals, a three-man bench ranked only by the United States Supreme Court.

"I understand that you feel you are right in the position you are taking and I sympathize with that position," Judge

about Judy Garland. As a result, Miss Garland last March filed in United States District Court a $1,393,333 breach of contract and libel suit against CBS.

Not a Defendant

Neither Miss Torre nor the Herald Tribune was named as a defendant. But according to Lionel S. Popkin, counsel for Miss Garland, "It's essential to our case (against CBS) that we know the name of the network executive of CBS who gave the statement to Miss Torre."

Mr. Popkin, of the law firm of Hess, Mela, Segall, Popkin & Gutterman, of 415 Madison Ave., has said "We need this because thus far we have been unable to ascertain the name of that network executive from two executives of CBS whom we have examined under oath before trial. They have denied knowing who gave the statement to Miss Torre."

It was during recent pretrial hearings that Miss Torre was asked to name that source —and she refused.

8G PHILLY REFUND AS JUDY MISSES 2 SHOWS

Philadelphia, Oct. 8.

Illness cut short Judy Garland's week stand at the Mastbaum Theatre, just as it had abbreviated her previous engagement in Washington, D.C. The singer missed the last two performances of her eight-show engagement and local Stanley Warner office was forced to make refunds of more than $8,000 to ticketholders.

House was heavily papered for the first two shows, with Jewish holidays cutting heavily into the expected take. Weekend biz picked up, however, and Stanley Warner execs hoped that the full run might gross $60,000, which would have allowed them a small margin of profit.

Miss Garland was at the Mastbaum on a straight percentage deal. Heavy exploitation plus band and costs of house found local sponsors in the red with total take running less than $46,000 for six

Old Dispute Crops Up to Mar
Judy Garland's Success at Met

The bitterness of a professional debacle returned today to mar the latest triumph of singer Judy Garland.

The value of the bitterness was put at $150,000 by night club operator Ben Maksik, who went to court in a move to attach her salary from the Metropolitan Opera.

The basis of the action is the dispute between the singer and Maksik last March, when her engagement at the Brooklyn Town and Country Club came to an abrupt halt.

Miss Garland said she was fired. Maksik said she walked out.

Court Order

A legal order preliminary to the attachment of Miss Garland's assets has been issued by Justice

Beckinella of Brooklyn Supreme Court.

Maksik said today:

"Service of the order has been accepted by her attorneys."

Miss Garland could not be reached for comment.

Benefit Performance

Miss Garland's run at the Met is a week-long benefit for the Children's Asthma Research Institute and Hospital in Denver. Her performance has been praised by the critics.

Maksik said the attachment was aimed only at Miss Garland's paycheck and "has nothing to do with the monies that would go to the children's charity fund."

He said the difficulties connected with her performance at the Brooklyn club "nearly ruined

my operation and jeopardized the jobs of nearly 300 persons."

"It drove my business into a reorganization from which we are only now beginning to recover," Maksik said.

"Now, we'll probably have a hearing on whether we have a right to sue for the $150,000. She's a non-resident and the cause of this action is to protect a resident of New York against a non-resident."

Maksik, whose club went through bankruptcy proceedings and eventual reorganization, said he had been unsuccessful in attempting to deal with Miss Garland's husband and manager, Sid Luft.

"Miss Garland and her husband have been ducking responsibility for years," he charged.

Judy Packs Hub Garden for Wow Take of $49,534

Boston, Oct. 31.

Judy Garland made history in Boston as the first femme performer solo to pack Boston Garden with its absolute 13,909-seat capacity, including seats behind the stage and obstructed perches. With a 32 piece orch and Mort Lindsay conducting, she pulled 12,597 paid customers and grossed $49,534 for the Friday (27) one-nighter.

Presented by Sid Bernstein & John Drew Jr., who did Music at Newport last summer, the show was considered a sellout as seats behind the stage are usually not sold, and a screen is put up in back of the stage. However, Eddie Powers, treasurer of the Garden, related, "due to terrific demand for seats it was decided to print the seats behind the stage."

Judy Garland Is Sick; Pill Overdose Denied

United Press International

CARSON CITY, Nev., Sept. 15—A doctor at Carson-Tahoe Hospital said today that entertainer Judy Garland is suffering from a kidney disease and flatly denied earlier reports that she took an accidental overdose of barbiturates.

Dr. Richard Grundy said the 39-year-old actress was suffering from acute pyelonephritis in her right kidney, which produces a severe pain similar to kidney stones. He said she would probably be able to leave the hospital within 48 hours.

Miss Garland was earlier believed to have been hospitalized for an accidental over-

JUDY GARLAND

GRABS KIDS, OFF FOR LONDON

Judy Flees Country

N. Y. MIRROR

APR 29 1962

By ROY METCALF

Pale and distraught, singer Judy Garland last night fled to London to prevent her estranged husband, Sid Luft, from snatching away their two children.

Three burly private detectives guarded Judy and the Luft children, Joey, 7, and Lorna, 9, as they boarded a jet at Idlewild. With them was Lisa Minelli, 16, her daughter by an earlier marriage to director Vincente Minelli.

The trip was so precipitate that Lisa was wearing slacks and sandals and had slips, dresses and sweaters draped over her arm. She told reporters she didn't have time to gather clothes for the trip.

JUDY, HOARSE from an attack of laryngitis, wouldn't elaborate on an earlier statement in which she said she was told Luft threatened to have her branded an unfit mother.

She had been slated to go to London in a few days to begin work on a new picture, "The Lonely Stage," but checked out of the Stanhope at Fifth Ave. and 81st St., unexpectedly.

"I am leaving for London ear-

Judy Garland Returning to Film Career

Singer-Actress Signed by Kramer

After a six-year absence from the screen, Judy Garland will return to films for an important dramatic role in Stanley Kramer's production of "Judgment at Nuremberg."

Miss Garland's signing was announced jointly by her and Mr. Kramer at a press conference yesterday at the Hotel Carlyle. In the film, scheduled to go before the cameras next month, Miss Garland will play Irene Hoffman, an "Aryan" German girl accused by the Germans of violating the Nuremberg race laws.

DAILY NEWS, N. Y.

Judy Garland, Exhausted, in Hospital Here

Judy Garland, exhausted after a long spell of film-

Judy Says Her New Marriage Is 'Absolutely Legitimate'

JUN 1 2 1964

Associated Press

HONG KONG, June 12—Judy Garland said today her marriage to her traveling companion, Mark Herron, is "absolutely legitimate."

In a gaily decorated suite aboard an American liner, the singer said she and actor Herron were married last Saturday aboard the Norwegian cargo ship Bodo three miles off this British colony.

Miss Garland, 41, and Her-

"This time it was a traditional Chinese ceremony with candles and joss sticks," she said.

Intimates of the singing star in Hollywood had termed earlier reports of her marriage "just a gag," saying that she had not been divorced from Sid Luft. They have been sep-

arated two years and lately have been in a battle for custody of their children.

"To the best of my knowledge she's still married to Sid Luft," said Fred Field, Judy's manager in Hollywood.

Herron said Miss Garland had obtained a Mexican divorce.

Judy and Her Fifth

Judy Garland, 46, and her fifth husband, Mickey Deans, 35, laugh it up in her nightclub dressing room in London after confirming their Jan. 9 marriage—first revealed exclusively by Post columnist Leonard Lyons on Jan. 15.

Associated Press Cablephoto

JUDY: *The Garland Cult*

Not in the history of show business has an entertainer inspired the kind of worship and adulation that Judy Garland receives from her loyal fans.

Most critics have stated that this incredible idolatry by Judy's audiences is an electrifying part of any Judy Garland show. It has been noted that the Garland Cult is composed not only of her contemporaries but also youngsters under twenty. The outpouring of love and affection from the audience for Judy establishes a rapport that no other entertainer has ever equaled.

One man—Wayne Martin—can be considered the "High Priest" of the Cult, a man who has literally devoted his entire life to following Judy Garland's career and assembling a collection of Garlandia over the past thirty-two years that is unequaled.

Many articles have been written on Mr. Martin and "Judyland," his "museum" of Garland memorabilia. Below is a reprint of an article which appeared in the *Los Angeles Times* in April, 1963.

JUDYLAND MUSEUM
Garland's Life Recorded by Fan

Los Angeles Times (Saturday, April 13, 1963)

In an apartment on Beachwood Drive a man lives alone with a dog and the collection of a lifetime—Judy Garland's lifetime.

From Wayne Martin's balcony you can see the larger-than-life letters that spell Hollywood across the hills. Inside his living room, which he calls Judyland, is the larger-than-life presence of Miss Garland. Photographs and posters pock-mark the walls. Scrapbooks and picture albums clutter the cabinets. Phonograph records and file cabinets fill up the tabletops. For 27 years, Martin has been the self-committed curator of the world's most complete personal museum. If Judy Garland claims the most rabid

With Wayne Martin after a radio broadcast of Easter Parade *in 1951*

responses of any star left in the system, then Martin of all fans is the inter-stellar champ.

Even a quick inventory is impressive: more than one dozen scrap books tracing Miss Garland from the time she was a little girl named Gumm in Minnesota to the present; one-half dozen photo albums plus stills from 29 motion pictures; programs from Garland live appearances; eight scripts; nearly 100 tapes, including 18 M-G-M movies, radio shows and television programs; recordings on all three speeds from the 30's to the present; paintings; even fragments of costumes.

Almost daily, the collection grows. Martin haunts the newsstand at Hollywood Boulevard and Las Palmas, researching and purchasing every new piece of Garland information, from item to interview. Studios send him any new photographs. His fellow fans from all over the country kindly send any bits and pieces that they find.

In 1936, at a late teen-age when most young men are moonstruck, Wayne Martin was already hopelessly star-struck. He saw a short subject with two young singers, one named Durbin, the other Garland. From then on, Judy became a preoccupation. "I took one

With Wayne Martin and Rock Hudson at the Cocoanut Grove in 1958

[213]

*With Maurice Chevalier and
Tony Perkins*

glimpse of this child and I was completely fascinated," admits
Martin. "I sensed there was a greatness there."

He submerged his spare time in the success of somebody else.
For the next 14 years, the star to whom he hitched his hobby
remained a total stranger. Then, in 1950, through the good offices
of CBS, Martin enjoyed the first of several short meetings with
Miss Garland. Dutifully, over the years, he has written to her.
Once in a while, she has answered in what Martin calls her left-
handed longhand. "Her friends have told me," he says, "that she
considers me about as old hat as family, that I shouldn't be
unhappy because she doesn't write more often."

His support has never wavered. "I've collected the good and the
bad. The whole legend of Garland is made up of many things,
including the illnesses and the heartaches." Martin says that he
always sensed a great strength and force in Judy; in times of
trouble, he sent her notes of cheer or religious faith.

Having seen her magic sooner than Judy's fans of today, Martin
has tried to define what inspires the frenzy and fanaticism of her
followers. "As soon as the overture starts, a feeling comes over the

whole audience—the anticipation and the love. When she sings, there's a cry from her being." Somewhere in that wail, thinks Martin, is the secret: people want to help her.

Giving so much to Garland over the years has cost him. Wistfully, Martin admits, "I have friends I love dearly and sometimes they show resentment for my concentration on Judy. I've had to explain two levels of affection." And others who may not have been resentful, were not respectful either. "I used to get a lot of kidding, but now that my collection has reached such proportions, people take it more seriously than they used to."

The Hollywood Museum has told Martin that it would be happy to have the Garland artifacts. He plans to make them a gift to the museum in a couple of years, believing that he can thereby share the treasures with other Judy followers while still adding and augmenting at home. . . .

Amidst the mementos, Wayne Martin appears to lead a tranquil, vicarious life. In a strange, semi-scholarly way, he has raised the standards of fandom at the same time he has sacrificed himself. He does not pester Judy, makes no demands upon her in return for his loyalty; all she must do is be.

Leaving the peculiar jumble of Judyland, one first feels pity for the thoughtful, gentle man inside. On second thought, Martin has more company than many other lonely people in this world. And maybe he is happier and less sick than many of us who, like his idol, are out there clashing and competing and making comebacks every day. (ART SEIDENBAUM)

JUDY: *Encore*

COMMENTS

ARTHUR FREED *comments:* Physically, I think the girl is made of iron. She's never going to fall apart physically. I don't think you've read the finish of Judy Garland yet. She'll come back. She's unpredictable—this girl will come back.

JOE PASTERNAK *comments:* I can say this—I don't think there will ever be another Judy Garland.

I think Judy has to keep on going, regardless—I think it's a matter of needing money to live. Even if Judy was financially able, I don't think she could stop. I think she'll keep on singing until they put her in her grave. It's an outlet. It's part of her life.

In various countries the government gives a pension to great artists. I think Judy did so much for America she should be paid by the government.

Judy Remembered

The first edition of this book was published on May 26, 1969. On June 22, 1969, at the age of forty-seven, Judy Garland died at her home in London.

Later that week at her funeral in New York, in a tribute unequaled since the time of Rudolph Valentino, more than 22,000 people came to pay their last respects to Judy. They proved that her tremendous following came from every age and walk of life. And *Variety* commented: "Even in the end, Judy Garland made show business history."

———

"Judy's great gift," James Mason said in his eulogy, "was that she could wring tears out of hearts of rock."

Ray Bolger said, "She doesn't have to sing 'Over the Rainbow' anymore. She has already sung it into your hearts."

———

There is no death
when you live in the hearts
of those you've left behind